Stories, Stats and Stuff
About Arkansas™ Basketball

By Dudley E. Dawson

Printed in the United States of America by
Mennonite Press, Inc.

ISBN 1-880652-72-2

PHOTO CREDITS All photographs were supplied
by the University of Arkansas and Andy Shupe.

ACKNOWLEDGMENTS

When undertaking this project, I had no idea just what a storied tradition that the University of Arkansas basketball program had in its past.

Sure Arkansas has the winningest college basketball program in the nation in the 1990s and has made three trips to the Final Four during that time, but it was very enlightening to find out just how successful the program became almost from its inception in 1923 under Francis Schmidt.

While researching the material for this book, that success made it very hard to decide what was more important than the other. That's why the first draft from this long-winded author had to have some 15,000 words deleted before it fit the publisher's desired length.

This book would not have been possible without my wife Laura Horne Dawson, who served as my research assistant and copy editor and No. 1 fan when the days and nights got long.

It also could not have happened without Lindsey, 8, and Brooks, 5, understanding how Dad needed to spend more time on the computer than they did during the summer.

Special thanks to the University of Arkansas sports information department, which allowed me to use photos and dig through mountains of material in researching the book.

I also could not have finished the project without the research materials at the University of Arkansas Library, truly a top-notch facility.

I would also be remiss without thanking Midwest Sports editor MeLinda Via, who one can tell is not only very good at what she does, but a very enjoyable person to deal with.

I hope you enjoy this look at the Razorbacks program, which I believe is presented in a easy-to-read fashion. Because of length constraints not everyone and everything associated with the program is included, but we did our best to hit on the high points — and there are plenty of them.

— *Dudley*

To my mom, Brenda, and dad, Ben, who instilled in me the value of hard work and to my brother Jeff, who has been a trusted friend.

INTRODUCTION

When most people think about Arkansas basketball, the names Nolan Richardson, Eddie Sutton, Sidney Moncrief, Joe Kleine, Todd Day and Corliss Williamson come to mind.

But this is a basketball program that flourished way before any of those men were born and continues today to have as great a degree of success as any program in the country.

From the five straight Southwest Conference titles in the 1920s to grabbing the last three regular-season and SWC Tournament titles handed out during Arkansas' stay in the league to bringing home a national title, there is plenty to share.

This is a program that once had four of the five members of the All-SWC team. It is one that teams feared playing because of the Razorbacks' high-scoring offense and pressure defense — in the 1920s as well as today.

The names are legendary. Johnny Adams' 36 points in one game in the 1930s was like a player scoring 70 in a game in the '90s.

George Kok, the first giant on campus, who ruled the paint like no one had before.

Then there were the Triplets — Parts 1, 2 and 3 — in each of the last three decades.

There were the vintage Arkansas-Texas games, where the sideline antics between first Abe Lemons and Sutton and then Richardson and Tom Penders sometimes overshadowed what happened on the court.

There were the Final Four trips to St. Louis, Denver, Charlotte and Seattle, events where Razorback fans flocked.

And who could forget Barnhill South, the annual trek of Arkansas fans to seemingly take over Reunion Arena and indeed all of Dallas one weekend each year in March.

Many outsiders often wonder why Arkansas fans put such fervor into their calling of the Hogs. After reading this book, you'll know why.

— *Dudley*

TABLE OF CONTENTS

Dirt Floors to National Champs

The high-arcing three-pointer that Arkansas sophomore Scotty Thurman launched over Duke senior Antonio Lang with 50.9 seconds left in the 1994 NCAA Championship game was more than just a shot that handed the school's basketball program it's first national title.

Indeed, as the ball tickled the twine and gave the Razorbacks an insurmountable advantage in the 76-72 victory, there were more than 72 years of hard work and memories nestling inside the net with it in Charlotte, N.C.

Dwight Stewart delivered the pass, Thurman nailed the shot and Nolan Richardson put the pieces of the puzzle together, but this was a moment to be shared equally by names like Francis Schmidt, George Kok, Sidney Moncrief and Todd Day.

Sports Illustrated published a commemorative issue on Arkansas' 1994 national championship season.

"What our kids accomplished that night, they accomplished for themselves, they accomplished for their teammates, they accomplished for this school and they accomplished for the fans of this great state who have been so loyal in their support over the years," Richardson said. "And they are all very aware that there were so many people who worked so hard to lay the foundation to make this possible."

All of them very aware of how the program went, literally, from a game played in a barn, to one played in a dust storm, to one played in one of the finest basketball facilities in the world.

A FOOTBALL TITLE, MAYBE That Arkansas was celebrating a national title in 1994 was not that big of a shock. But what stunned many old-timers was that the national title came in a sport other than football.

Razorback alumni and fans proudly talk of their 1964 National Championship football team, one coached by the legendary Frank Broyles that featured a couple of players named Jerry Jones and Jimmy Johnson, a pair who would go on to build a dynasty with the NFL's Dallas Cowboys.

"For the longest, football was the only thing we had going that we could really sink our resources into," said Broyles, who has been the athletic director since retiring as coach in the 1970s. "Basketball at Arkansas was strong for many, many years until they kind of ran out of money and we had just enough money to have a football program. Basketball was still financially supported, but nothing the likes of what it should have been."

At a school that has been known as a football factory and where brilliant track coach John McDonnell — he of the 26 NCAA indoor, outdoor and cross country

Winningest programs of the 1990s
(through 1995-96)

School	Victories
1. Arkansas	195
2. Kansas	194
3. N. Carolina	184
(tie) Kentucky	184
5. Massachusetts	183

Former Arkansas football coach Frank Broyles brought Nolan Richardson to Arkansas.

national titles — adds yearly to his unbelievable total, this basketball success was still the biggest thing to hit Arkansas in a long time.

"The championship gave Arkansas people something to rally around," Broyles said. "People enjoy supporting and being involved in something like that because you have proven you can do something better than anybody else. That's a goal of everybody. Everybody's ambition is — whether you are a farmer or whatever — you want to be better than anybody else and we were."

IT REALLY DID START IN A BARN Heading into the 1996-97 season, Arkansas is the winningest college basketball team in the 1990s and plays in Bud Walton Arena, a $35 million dollar basketball palace that rivals any college or professional arena in the country.

That's a long way from the Razorbacks' first home, which was affectionately dubbed Schmitty's Barn.

Francis Schmidt started the basketball program in 1922 by rounding up some of the football standouts and local YMCA basketball stars on campus at the time.

But there was no facility to house the program until Schmidt scraped enough money together to buy a barn-like structure, get it moved, and have it reshaped around a basketball court.

The first of Arkansas' two "barns" was home to the Razorbacks for a dozen years, but the Razorbacks soon moved into the Men's Gym, their home until 1970.

The 1970s brought Barnhill Arena, which is where the Razorbacks played their basketball games but was more important to the athletic department as an indoor

Francis Schmidt

Schmitty's Barn was the Razorbacks' first home.

FRANK J. ROONEY INC.

training facility for the ultra-successful football program and housing for the athletic offices.

Often times the basketball players ended practice covered in sawdust and dirt, which flew on them as the football team went through spring football drills in a sawdust workout area and the track team raced around the dirt track just off the court.

This was not what Eddie Sutton had in mind when Broyles was trying to hire him as head coach in 1974. In fact, Sutton was promised changes would be made before he agreed to sign on.

Soon enough Barnhill Arena was turned into a

Arkansas' famed Triplets led the Razorbacks over Notre Dame in the NCAA's last third-place game in 1978.

Eddie Sutton took Arkansas basketball to new heights after being hired in 1974.

basketball-only facility and seating expanded from 5,000 to 9,000.

"Eddie sat in my office and said 'We've got to have a new facility,' " Broyles said. "I said 'I promise you that we will get you a new facility.' That old theory of build it and they will come happened because he started winning his first year and the excitement took off and hadn't slowed down since."

That has a lot to do with Richardson, who has taken the program to a level far removed from the "barn-like structure." The Razorbacks now play their games before sellout crowds of more than 20,000 per game at Bud Walton Arena.

SCHMITTY'S BARN

Francis Schmidt had plenty of things to do when he started the Razorback basketball program in 1923, but as important as any task was finding a place for his team to play.

There was no suitable venue on campus, a plight that prompted Schmidt to take matters into his own hands. With the University's permission, he began a fundraising campaign to purchase what was described as a "barn-like structure."

He then had the barn-like structure moved and reshaped around a basketball court to give Arkansas a home for its practice games in 1922-23 and its first official season in 1923-24.

The Razorbacks' first official game in Schmitty's Barn was played on Dec. 19, 1923, with the hosts prevailing 16-13 over Tahlequah Teachers College (now Northeastern Oklahoma State).

Arkansas was successful in

Schmitty's Barn

SO CLOSE BUT YET SO FAR Arkansas spent a lot time traveling down the road to a national title, but took a few exits before arriving at the promised land.

The Razorbacks earned four berths to the eight-team NCAA Tournament in the 1940s, but perhaps missed their best chance in 1944 when a tragic car wreck kept them from going. Oregon subbed for Arkansas and won the national title.

Sutton, then an Oklahoma State star, made sure Arkansas' trip to the 1958 NCAA Western Regional was an unsuccessful one. The Razorbacks' only trip to the fore-runner of the Big Dance ended with future NBA star Oscar Robertson pouring in 58 points in a consolation game.

Ron Brewer led the Razorbacks to the 1978 Final Four.

Schmitty's Barn as it won SWC championships in seven (1926, 1927, 1928, 1929, 1930, 1935 and 1936) of the 13 seasons it played in the facility.

As Arkansas' basketball team racked up championships and enhanced its popularity, the fact that Schmitty's Barn had a capacity of only 1,350 became a problem.

The fact that the University had 1,750 students at the time — almost all of whom wanted to attend the games — meant that some 400 at a time would not be able to attend.

Francis Schmidt presents a trophy to future Razorback Ralph Hazlip and his District 1 high school championship team March 24 inside Schmitty's Barn, the Razorback basketball program's first home.

1. What Arkansas coach was also the school's first basketball All-American?

It took Sutton — the coach — to get the Razorbacks' next ticket to the NCAA, a feat that occurred some 19 years later.

Although exiting in the first round, the Razorbacks had all five starters coming back and found themselves in the Final Four in 1978 at The Checkerdome in St. Louis.

The Razorbacks lost to eventual champion Kentucky, but did down Notre Dame on Ron Brewer's last-second shot in the last third-place game ever played in the NCAA tournament.

The Razorbacks would not see the Final Four again until Richardson arrived. A 30-5 team led by current NBA players Todd Day, Lee Mayberry and Oliver Miller ended up in the 1990 quartet in Denver, setting the stage for the 1994 theatrics.

IT FINALLY HAPPENS Little was expected from Arkansas in 1994, but the Razorbacks raced through the SEC and marched to Charlotte behind the efforts of Thurman, fellow sophomore Corliss Williamson and several junior standouts like Corey Beck.

President Bill Clinton and Arkansas coach Nolan Richardson celebrate after a win in Bud Walton Arena in 1994.

The 31-3 Razorbacks whipped North Carolina A&T, Georgetown, Tulsa, Michigan and Arizona before tangling for the title with Duke.

"It was a magical year, but one that was borne out of a lot of hard work and commitment," Richardson said. "It set off one big celebration that really hasn't stopped."

THEY REALLY ARE STILL CELEBRATING In a state where there is no professional sports franchise, only one major university and a group of citizens who have been ridiculed in the past by the national media for their perceived simple nature, the national title has been revered more than most.

Sales of 1994 shirts, caps and other championship paraphernalia was still going strong in 1996 — bolstered by sales when Arkansas returned to the NCAA championship game in 1995.

Broyles notes he has never seen anything like it, but knows exactly why the fans worship this success so much.

"It was the most important significant rallying point of people in our state," Broyles said. "Some of them had become lukewarm. The rabid fans were always there, but we joined forces with the lukewarm fans and those who had not even supported the Razorbacks, maybe, in far corners of the state into a statewide mania. It just took off and it still exists today."

Top 5 Active Coaches
(through 1995-96)
1. Jerry Tarkanian, Fresno State, 643-133 (.829)
2. Roy Williams, Kansas, 213-56 (.792)
3. Dean Smith, North Carolina, 850-247 (.775)
4. Jim Boeheim, Syracuse, 483-159 (.752)
5. Nolan Richardson, Arkansas, 391-132 (.748)

Early Influences

THE FRANCIS SCHMIDT ERA

Francis Schmidt started the Arkansas basketball program and led the Razorbacks to four straight SWC titles.

The 1994 national championship certainly would not have happened if a man name Francis Schmidt had not come along and literally built the program from the ground up.

Schmidt, a native of Downs, Kan., who had been a football star for Nebraska, came to Arkansas from bitter rival Tulsa, where he had developed a flamboyant, high-scoring style of offensive football.

In fact, in Schmidt's first game as head coach at Tulsa, the Golden Hurricane bombed Oklahoma Baptist 152-0, which is still the school's most lopsided victory ever.

His Tulsa teams averaged 50 points from 1919 through 1921 while giving up just four a game.

MR. PERFECTION It was just a classic example of how the man was always striving for perfection. Everywhere he went he carried a notepad and a pocket full of pencil stubs.

He carried the pencil stubs because he thought he would never have to worry about anybody stealing them. He also used different colors — blue for the ball carrier, red for the blockers and green for the pass receivers.

He wasted nothing, especially not paper.

The Razorbacks' first home was Schmitty's Barn.

"He once wrote me a letter," legendary football great Sid Gillman said. "When I opened the envelope, I

couldn't find anything inside. Then all of a sudden, before I threw it away, there was a note to me on the flap just above where you seal it."

It was this attention to detail that Schmidt used when he decided to start a basketball program at the University of Arkansas in 1922. He rounded up several of the more athletic football players and also grabbed players on YMCA teams in Fayetteville and other towns.

Perhaps most importantly, Schmidt raised money to buy a barn-like structure, move it and place it around a basketball court to give Arkansas its first home: Schmitty's Barn.

The Razorbacks played several informal games in 1922-23 before jumping headlong into Southwest Conference play a year later.

RAZORBACK QUIZ

2. Arkansas' first two basketball victories were against the same team. Name that team.

GETTING THE BARN IN ORDER After leading the football team to a successful campaign, Schmidt gathered up a freshman basketball team and began to schedule exhibition games.

The first Arkansas cagers were listed as forwards "Big" Charles Corgan, Rolla Adams, Elbert Pickell, guards Elza Renfro, Curtis Parker and Clifford Blackburn, center Tom Williams and a reserve who never lettered who was referred to in team records only as the "lanky Brown."

The first exhibition game was the back end of a tripleheader against Keota (Okla.) High School, which followed two games between intramural teams.

The *Fayetteville Daily Democrat* — which is now known as the *Northwest Arkansas Times* — announced the event this way in its Jan. 11, 1923, edition:

"Local basketball fans will have an opportunity to spend the day witnessing their favorite sport on Saturday of this week … At 3 o'clock, the Freshman will be pitted against the Keoto, Oklahoma, high school.

"Dr. Gronnert, former basketball coach for Centre College, will referee the Freshman-Keota game."

The Jan. 12 *Fayetteville Daily Democrat* told of a rousing win for the Freshmen in a game that was refereed by Schmidt and in which assistant coach Ivan Grove served as timekeeper.

"The Freshman basketball squad defeated the Keota High School team by the score of 20 to 15 at the University this afternoon. This is the first defeat that the visitors had suffered this year, having defeated Fort Smith in two games yesterday."

RAZORBACK QUIZ

3. What Arkansas player led the nation in free throw shooting in 1974-75?

1923-24: THE FIRST OFFICIAL SEASON Schmidt's first team found the early going fairly easy, even if the offensive outputs paled in comparison to Schmidt's football teams.

The school's first official game was a 16-13 win at

Razorbacks Win From Tahlequah By 16-13 Score

The Fayetteville Daily Democrat, Dec. 19, 1923.

what is now called Northeastern Oklahoma State on Dec. 19, 1923. It was not without controversy as the Fayetteville paper reported the following day.

"Arkansas University won its first official basketball game Wednesday night when the squad humbled the Tahlequah Indians, at Tahlequah by the close score of 16 to 13. The game was so rough that the referee resigned at the half and the Tahlequah coach had to take up the burden of officiating."

Adams, J.C. McGuire, Pickell, Parker and Renfro made up the school's first official starting five.

The Razorbacks were 17-11 in their first campaign, but a 3-9 mark in SWC action put them in the basement of the seven-team league.

THE FIRST OF MANY 20-WIN SEASONS While the Razorbacks were still roughing up such "powerhouses" as Gay Oil Company, England National Bank and the Stuttgart Athletic Club, their second season also marked a noticeable improvement in league play.

Arkansas finished third by winning 10 of its 14 SWC games in its second year, setting the stage for a dramatic worst to first improvement in just a three-year span.

A 21-5 season included scoring an unheard of 78 points in a game and a split with Oklahoma A&M, the beginning contests in what would turn into a hotly contested series over the years.

Rolla Adams became the school's first all-conference player, but Arkansas lost both games to Texas.

The Razorbacks finished third in the SWC that year, but actually went into the final game with a chance to tie for the title with a win over then-SWC member Oklahoma A&M.

Oklahoma A&M claimed the title by scoring six points in the final two minutes for a 25-23 win.

RAZORBACK QUIZ

4. What is the highest total of points a Razorback team has scored in a game?

1925-26: THE FIRST CHAMPIONSHIP Schmidt waved his magic wand and led his third team to a SWC championship just two years after beginning the program.

The Razorbacks were 23-2 overall and raced through the league with an 11-1 record, the only loss a 30-15 defeat at the hands of TCU in the season's last game after the league crown had already been decided.

This team was so good that it had four of the five members of the All-SWC team in Adams, Pickell, Parker and standout newcomer Glen Rose.

The Razorbacks outscored their opponents 347-184

Former standouts Elbert Pickell (left) and Glen Rose are shown here at a get-together in 1935 to talk about their old playing days.

and rolled up a 9-1 record early on while "barnstorming all over the state and a good part of the country" via train.

Porkers Again Defeat Texas

The Fayetteville Daily Democrat, Feb. 7, 1926

TAKING DOWN THE LONGHORNS This team also went on to do something very important to the people of Arkansas as it started a stretch where it would reel off five straight SWC championships — it swept Texas (35-12 and 27-7).

Pickell had 17 points in the opening game to outscore the entire Longhorn club by himself in the 35-12 victory on Feb. 5, the first ever over Texas.

The *Fayetteville Daily Democrat* could hardly contain itself in its report after the win.

"The Razorbacks made history here Friday night when for the first time they humbled their ancient enemy, the University of Texas.

Arkansas holds an 85-64 advantage in its series with rival Texas.

"A record crowd of 1,500 saw the tilt. And they cheered and cheered and cheered. It was basketball homecoming and all available space in the gym was taken.

"The score was 35 to 12 but the game was better and harder than the score would indicate. The Longhorns are a bunch of long boys — these fellows that came here from Texas — but they were pitted against a real team that also claims a long one or two. And the Porkers showed them a game of teamwork — fast rushing, accurate shooting and effective defense."

SEALING THE DEAL Arkansas would go on to clinch the conference title with a four-game road swing through Texas in which it dropped Rice twice and handled Texas A&M in a pair of contests.

The Razorbacks downed TCU, 24-23, the final weekend of the season when a last-second Horned Frog shot was off, but the "Toads" dumped Arkansas, 30-15, to ruin the perfect SWC campaign.

THE RUN CONTINUES The Razorbacks were 14-2 overall and 8-2 in 1926-27, on their way to taking the SWC title over Rice, TCU, Texas A&M, Texas and SMU. Arkansas did not play either Baylor or SMU that season.

The school's second straight SWC title came as a surprise to many as Arkansas was thought to be rebuilding and picked no higher than fourth by the experts. A season review in the following year's program gave this account:

Harold Steele was captain of the 1926-27 squad.

"Taking a squad composed of an equal amount of veterans and untried men, Schmidt constructed a team around captain Harold Steele and Glen Rose, a quintet that met but two defeats the entire season.

"Six of the stars of the previous championship were gone and it appeared as if nothing short of a miracle would maintain the Razorbacks at the top. The miracle happened and the team swept through a six-game preliminary season undefeated.

"Still the conference critics did not enthuse over our prospects. But the undaunted Razorbacks, led by Harold Steele, the brilliant (Ralph) Hazlip and the sensational Tom Pickell, and supported by big Glen Rose and sub-captain Harold Burk, swept to six consecutive victories before being stopped temporarily by the Texas Longhorns.

"But the fighting spirit again asserted itself and the

Ralph Hazlip, left, and Tom Pickell, middle, were early Razorback standouts.

Byran Gregory, right, hit a game-winning shot against SMU.

squad turned in two straight victories over the SMU Mustangs and clinched the title."

Steele, Rose and Pickell were named all-conference. Arkansas had to go to Texas without star guard Gene Lambert and ended up losing two bitterly fought games to put its conference title hopes in jeopardy.

But with the conference title riding on the line, the Razorbacks regrouped and headed to SMU on the same road trip. A sensational field goal by forward Bryan Gregory in the closing minutes of the final game sealed the victory and handed Arkansas the league crown.

THE FIRST ALL-AMERICAN Glen Rose, who would later go on to be a great football and basketball coach at his alma mater, made history by becoming the school's first All-American in 1927-28 as the team went 19-1, including a 12-0 SWC mark.

The Razorbacks — who one writer said "swept through the conference like a rabid Razorback through a Texas turkey ranch" — ran up a new school scoring record of 470 points and were hailed as the greatest SWC

The 1928-29 SWC champs made it four in a row for Arkansas.

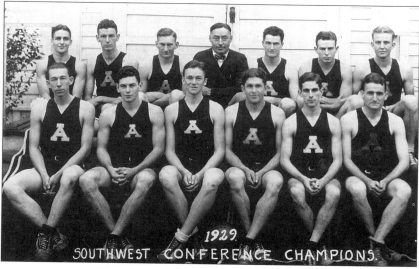

1929.
SOUTHWEST CONFERENCE CHAMPIONS.

Glen Rose proved to be a winner both as a player and a coach at Arkansas.

Gene Lambert was another early star who would go on to coach at Arkansas.

team to that point.

Rose was named all-conference for the third straight year while Pickell , Gene Lambert and Wear "Jake" Schoonover were also on the All-SWC squad.

The Razorbacks finished their 12-0 march through the SWC with another four-game swing through Texas, with stops at Rice and Texas A&M.

1928-1929: SCHMIDT'S LAST HURRAH Sir Francis took the Razorbacks to their fourth straight crown and a second straight 19-1 campaign before leaving to take the head coaching post at TCU.

The Razorbacks had the talent to win its fourth straight championship, but they noticed right away that they would have to win four road games in five days to open the conference season to do so.

Arkansas did just that — whipping SMU and TCU twice and then downing Baylor in a game that featured Arkansas scoring an SWC-record 71 points and referees calling an unheard of 70 fouls.

That set up a two-game home set with Texas. While awaiting that showdown, it became known that Schmidt had accepted an offer to coach football at TCU next season. The coach was not vilified for his decision and instead got a glowing endorsement from Fayetteville writer Jim Bohart in his column called "Squealings."

"Texas gained where Arkansas has lost. He is a great believer in fundamentals and his players spend many hours in perfecting themselves in stops and turns, pivots, jumping, passing and shooting. He uses both a slow and a fastbreaking offense and his teams are extremely tricky. The opposition never knows what to expect."

The Razorbacks whipped Texas, 48-32, in the opening game and suffered their only defeat of the season at the hands of the Longhorns the next night.

Arkansas locked up its fourth straight crown by downing Texas A&M, 38-29, in Schmitty's Gym, in the UA mentor's final game.

THE CHARLES BASSETT ERA

Following the first basketball coaching legend at Arkansas was the job of Dr. Charles "Chuck" Bassett, who took over where Schmidt left off in part because of a strong returning cast led by Wear Schoonover and captain Jim Pickren.

Bassett had been in charge of the Arkansas football team's offensive line before taking over the hoop duties in 1929, and former standout Glen Rose was now in charge of the freshman team.

After an early season scrimmage, Bassett pronounced

his team ready to make a run for a fifth straight SWC title.

"We look darn good for the shape we are in right now," Bassett told the press in December. "After a little bit more practice, we should really be something."

One thing that took time to get used to was a different style of play. Unlike Schmidt's fast-breaking style of play, Bassett preferred a slow-breaking aggregation with the loss of offense compensated for by better defense.

With Schoonover and Pickren heading things up, the Razorbacks looked to be rolling at 4-0 before losing five straight to Missouri and Oklahoma teams as Bassett experimented with the lineup.

He found out what he needed just in time for the conference season, which saw Arkansas rip through the league with a 10-2 mark for its fifth straight title.

The Razorbacks swept non-conference foe Oklahoma State as well as league rivals TCU (with Schmidt aboard), Baylor, SMU and Texas A&M. Their only losses were in

The 1929-30 team won the school's fifth straight SWC crown with a slower-tempo offense.

Wear Schoonover, left, and Jim Pickren, middle, were two of the top stars during Bassett's coaching tenure.

Roy Prewitt, right, was named to the All-SWC team in 1930.

splits with Texas and Rice, the latter coming after they had already wrapped up the title.

Schoonover made it three straight years on the All-SWC squad and was joined by Razorback teammates Milan Creighton and Roy Prewitt. Pickren and Ken Holt were named second-team All-SWC.

THE TITLE RUN ENDS All good things must come to an end and that's just what happened with the 1930-31 Razorback squad, which finished 14-9 overall and tied for third in the SWC with a 7-5 mark.

Milan Creighton was another all-league pick.

Milan Creighton earned All-SWC honors for a second straight year during 1930-31, but the Razorbacks faltered down the stretch after splitting with Texas and sweeping Rice and Texas A&M to open the conference season 5-1.

A two-game sweep by TCU at Fort Worth started the beginning of the end and splitting series with Baylor and SMU were not good enough.

It appeared the 1931-32 team would take a step back toward the top of the conference after reeling off five straight wins to open the season behind the play of all-conference performers Doc Sexton and Tom Murphy.

The Razorbacks finished 18-6 overall and 8-4 in SWC action, but that was only good enough for third.

Bassett's final team in 1932-33 was 14-7 overall, but just fourth in league action with a 6-6 mark as Murphy was tabbed All-Conference again.

THE FIRST GLEN ROSE ERA

There was lots of excitement around campus when former basketball standout Glen Rose, who had been coaching the freshman team, was elevated to head up the varsity beginning with the 1933-34 season.

It would be the first of two highly successful tenures for Rose, who would win 323 games in his 23-year career at the helm of the Razorbacks.

Glen Rose would win 325 games in two stints as the boss at Arkansas.

Local newspaper reports heralded the hiring of Rose, but their optimism for his success was tempered by the sub-par campaigns the Razorbacks had experienced the past few seasons.

"Although Glen Rose, the University of Arkansas' first varsity coach who is a graduate of the institution, is optimistic, fans and students shouldn't expect too much from the cagers of 1933-34," noted the Fayetteville newspaper on Dec. 12, 1933.

"Not since the first season of varsity play in 1924 has an Arkansas quintet finished below a .500 percent average in the Southwest Conference … but the majority of close observers agree that they will have to battle every minute like no other Porker quintet has done before."

The Razorbacks finished 16-8 that year, but had to beat Baylor, 39-30, in the regular-season finale to get their SWC mark to an even 6-6.

Arkansas' top player was Taft Moody, one of the few veterans on the team. He would earn All-SWC honors while scoring 218 points in the 22 games he played.

The team also featured a talented sophomore forward in H.L. "Ike" Poole, who tallied 180 points, but the season might have been more noted for the defense of players like captain Travis Brasfield, Paul Rucker, Elstner Beall, Jack Newby and Elbert Cunningham.

The 1933-34 Razorback team was 16-8.

1934-35: BACK ON TOP AGAIN
It only took Rose two years to keep the string alive of every Arkansas coach capturing at least one SWC title.

The Razorbacks (14-5) stumbled out of the gate, but with All-SWC selections Moody and Poole leading the charge, the Razorbacks roared down the stretch to capture the league crown.

Arkansas' 9-3 mark, which included a three-game losing streak during the middle of the season, was good enough to top its league rivals. The Razorbacks closed things out in grand style by thumping Texas A&M, 51-31, at home.

1935-36: ONE OF THE BEST EVER
Rose's third team proved it was truly one of the best — if not the best — teams in school history while rolling up a 24-3 overall record, winning the SWC with an 11-1 mark and competing in the Olympic playoffs.

Six-foot-five Jim Lee Howell, Gilliland and Poole were the key cogs as the Razorbacks won 10 of their first 11 games, including grabbing a split with Oklahoma State, but found themselves tied with Texas for the SWC lead when Rice upset them four games into the conference slate.

Arkansas responded by winning it next eight games

Ike Poole became the school's fourth All-American with his play in 1935-36.

Don Lockard made his hometown of Batesville proud with a game-winning basket against Texas in 1935-36.

— six of them league tilts — to set up a winner-take-all situation between the two in Fayetteville the last week of the regular season.

The Razorbacks could clinch the crown with just one win in the series while the Longhorns would not only have to sweep Arkansas, but beat Texas A&M at College Station to claim the title.

The game lived up to its billing with sophomore Don Lockard of Batesville putting in the final two of his eight second-half points inside the last minute of the game. They were the decisive points in Arkansas' 38-37 win.

A REBUILDING AND BUILDING EFFORT Lockard finally got his due in 1937 when he was named All-Conference along with Jack Robbins on a rebuilding team that went 12-6 overall and finished second in the SWC at 8-4

But as the *Fayetteville Daily Democrat's* Jim Bohart noted in his preseason preview, the biggest news that year might have been the construction of the Men's Gymnasium going up near Schmitty's Barn.

"Less than 100 yards away from Schmitty's Barn construction is underway on a new field house that will seat enough fans not to require those desiring to see the cagers to miss their dinner and go through their turnstiles around 6:15 o'clock," Bohart wrote while also noting admission would be $1.10.

PACKING THEM IN The popularity of basketball at the University Arkansas rose to new heights when a record crowd of 2,750 fans poured into the new Men's Gymnasium for a SWC-title clinching win over Baylor in 1937-38.

Fans had packed the new venue all year as Lockard and Robbins again had All-SWC seasons while leading the Razorbacks (19-3, 11-1) to a second straight SWC title.

It was the Razorbacks eighth championship in 15 years and Coach Rose's fifth, three as a player and two as a coach.

The most interesting trip of the year was a train jaunt to Baylor that took 21 hours more than the Razorbacks had planned and forced the games to be moved back a day.

"Everything is all right except for two nights and two days on a train and a lot of bad colds," Rose assessed on the team's arrival, which was held up because of floods in Oklahoma.

Baylor took advantage of the tired Arkansas team to hand the Razorbacks a 54-47 loss, the only blemish on their league mark.

That loss and a good night's rest roused the visitors,

Lockard went on to star for the Phillips 66ers, an AAU power.

who whipped Baylor, 54-45, the following night.

The Razorbacks then drummed SMU to claim the championship.

THE NATURAL The 1938-39 campaign was highlighted by a great season from newcomer John Adams, a 6-3 sophomore guard who was described as a natural for the game.

Adams led the league in scoring and was named All-SWC.

"Basketball is my game," Adams said in an interview early on in season. "I love basketball and I live it and no matter how many points I score or how well I play, it still isn't enough."

One of his better games during a 18-5 season (in which the Razorbacks tied for the second in the SWC with a 9-3 mark) was a 22-point performance against Texas.

The Razorbacks had lost three straight — including one to the Longhorns — before Adams' offensive explosion led his team to a 65-41 thumping of Arkansas' bitter rival.

His performance spurred on his teammates, a crew made up mostly of sophomores who won its final 10

John Adams was the school's most offensively gifted performer ever when he arrived on campus.

THE MEN'S GYM

With help from federal works money in the mid-1930s, Arkansas basketball fans finally got a little more room with the arrival of the Men's Gymnasium.

The Men's Gymnasium, opened for the 1936-37 season, could crowd in as many as 2,500 fans since University of Arkansas officials allowed students to crowd around the court for many games.

The new seats got all of the students that wanted to attend the games into the event, but still was not big enough to open the contests to the general public.

Perhaps the biggest plus provided by the Men's Gymnasium was the fact that it solved the problem of having to come nearly two hours before the 8 p.m. tip-off just to get a seat.

The *Fayetteville Daily Democrat*

reported this was a problem that a group of dinner-preparing mothers had complained about vehemently before the construction of the new facility.

"Less than 100 yards away from Schmitty's Barn, construction is underway on a new field house that will seat enough fans not to require those desiring to see the cagers to miss their dinner and go through the turnstiles around 6:15 o'clock," reported the paper.

The Men's Gymnasium, not given a name for the longest, was Arkansas' home for more than 20 years. The Razorbacks won the SWC crown in the venue's first season and also racked up four more titles before moving on to a "new barn."

Howard Hickey was Arkansas' lone All-SWC pick in 1939-40.

games of the season.

Another top player was 6-foot-8 sophomore John Freiberger, who was effective and would have been even more effective had the center jump after each basket not been eliminated.

Sophomore Howard Hickey, who would go on to play in the NFL, was also an offensive force on a team that looked like it would be a powerhouse for the next two seasons.

OH, BROTHER! AN INJURY Arkansas was already struggling at 3-3 in 1939-40 when Adams came up lame. That left the team looking at its worst conference mark since the school's very first squad.

The Razorbacks had to sweep a season-ending series with visiting TCU to save the season. Howard Hickey, the only Razorback named to the All-SWC team, came through. He powered Arkansas to two wins over the

A SHOT AT THE OLYMPICS

Support reached a fever pitch in 1936 when the Arkansas basketball team downed visiting rival Texas and — with SWC title in tow — made a run at representing the United States in the 1936 games in Berlin.

The run was not without controversy, which could actually be looked upon as the first skirmish between the University of Arkansas and University of Kentucky basketball programs.

After Arkansas (22-4) traveled 650 miles to Austin, Texas, to win the District 4 tournament, it was told it would be playing Western Kentucky.

This upset Razorback officials because legendary University of Kentucky coach Adolph Rupp, the selection chairman of District 3, deemed Western Kentucky (30-3) the representative without a tournament.

Rupp stood his ground saying this was the interpretation he had been given by Olympic basketball chairman A.A. Schabinger of Chicago.

Arkansas stood its ground as well and worked out a deal where the playoff games moved from Memphis to Little Rock.

The games were anti-climatic as Arkansas roared to a 43-36 victory in the first game that had Rose saying this series "would only take two games and my boys are already looking forward to that tough final round in New York City."

It didn't seem that Western Kentucky coach Ed Diddle disagreed much with that stance, citing a Razorback crowd of 1,500 that rooted on the Razorbacks.

"My boys became a little flustered in the first part of the second half and couldn't quite make up the difference after that," said Diddle, admitting that the long one-handed shots by the Porker cagers were disheartening to his players.

Arkansas grabbed a 39-30 win the next night to earn a berth to play in the Olympic finals at

Horned Frogs to give Arkansas a 6-6 league mark, which was good enough for fourth.

1940-41: TALL AND EXPERIENCED

One of the most experienced and certainly the tallest Razorback teams in school history to this point rampaged unbeaten through the SWC with a 12-0 mark and ended the season 20-3 overall.

Senior John Adams, who would be named to the All-America team, was back and healthy while senior John Freiberger had taken on the nickname "Treetop" and was looking to put up his best numbers ever.

Hickey made it three seniors in the starting lineup, which averaged 6-foot-4 and also featured juniors O'Neal Adams and R.C. Pitts.

"They are the greatest college team I ever saw," SMU coach Whitey Baccus said.

An early season showdown at Texas opened the

RAZORBACK QUIZ

5. What Arkansas point guard played in more Razorback games thany any other player?

Madison Square Garden in New York City.

Rose took his entire 10-man squad to New York to face a field that included DePaul, the University of Washington, the McPherson (Kan.) Refiners, the Denver Safeways, Temple, Utah State and the Hollywood Universals.

The Razorbacks, playing before an overwhelming crowd of more than 12,000 fans, twice jumped out to leads in their opening round game with the Hollywood Universals.

But an 11-point lead early on and a one-point second-half lead failed to hold up and the AAU team came out on top, 40-29, by game's end.

Lockard had eight points and Robbins seven for Arkansas in the loss, which closed the Razorbacks' season. The Razorbacks did get a special treat before coming back when they had lunch at Jack Dempsey's restaurant.

"It was a nice experience for us all," said Rose. "We just wish we could have played better."

The 1935-36 team, which came close to representing its country in the Olympics, enjoys an off-the-court moment.

Gordon Carpenter was the star of the 1942-43 Razorback outfit.

conference season and Arkansas rallied from a first-half deficit to capture a 50-38 win.

A 44-34 win over the Longhorns the following night gave the Razorbacks their first-ever sweep in Austin.

"Take a walk, Old Man Jinx," Rose said after the wins tied the all-time series record at 18-18.

TOPPING THE CHARTS The victories against Texas proved to be a coming out party for sensational sophomore Gordon Carpenter, who poured in 20 points in the first game for a team that was picking up believers.

"The Razorbacks have one of the best records in Arkansas' basketball history and are probably the best team to ever grace that school," Carl Kay Bell wrote in the Feb. 17, 1941, *Fayetteville Daily Democrat.*

Arkansas was indeed ranked No. 1 among college teams at the time and entered a rubber game with the Phillips 66ers in position to take the top position over the semi-pros as well.

The two teams met in a charity game at Tulsa that raised money to replace some recently burned Tulsa playground equipment.

The top individual matchup featured former Razorback Don Lockard and current Arkansas standout John Adams, but the pair was held to a combined 13 points.

The Razorbacks led 17-16 at one point, but the older defending national AAU champs used their experienced down the stretch to take a 31-26 win.

ON TO THE NCAA The Razorbacks responded by reeling off four straight conference wins to complete a spotless 12-0 campaign.

One of those wins was a 67-42 pasting of TCU in which Adams poured in 36 points, a remarkable number then and today that set an SWC record. His 206 points overall was just four shy of the all-time SWC record.

That brought the Razorbacks invitations to both the NIT and NCAA tournaments, but the Razorbacks chose an NCAA Western Regional first-round date with Wyoming in Kansas City.

RAZORBACK QUIZ

6. What is the most lopsided loss in school history?

Adams scored 26 points and the Razorbacks bounced the Cowboys, 52-40, to set up a game with Washington State, which downed Creighton 48-39 in its opener.

While Arkansas was heavily favored and regarded as the best college team in the land, an off night and a scrappy Washington State ended the Razorbacks' campaign, 64-53, before a crowd of 8,000.

"Pardon us while we reach for the crying towel," Carl Kay Bell wrote in his column the next day. "If you see any tears mingled with these lines, you may rest assured that they did not come from the eyes of Coach John Friel or any of the Washington State Cougars.

"Arkansans weren't the only ones that surprised by their upsetting defeat of the Razorbacks in this National Athletic Association Western Finals Saturday night. Some 8,000 fans who witnessed the battle nearly fell out of their seats as the aces topped the highly rated Porkers, gaining the distinction of being the only college team to turn the trick this season."

SMELLING LIKE A ROSE With Adolph Hitler's antics dominating the front pages of newspapers in 1941, Razorback coach Glen Rose had some idea that 1941-42 might be the final year of his first tenure at Arkansas because he was also a top military officer.

He finished up in grand style by leading his team to a 19-4 overall record and a share of its second straight league crown.

Rose did so without some of the key cogs that had led the Razorbacks to so much success a season before. Gone were John Adams, Freiberger and Hickey. Rose also had to start the season without Carpenter, who underwent an appendectomy and was expected to miss at least half the season.

"Coach Glen Rose has long been called 'Gloomy Glen,' but if you catch Rose today you will find him sporting the saddest face of all time," cautioned the Fayetteville paper. "The wily mentor must build an entirely new team this year."

Things almost got worse when senior O'Neal Adams was called to Kansas City to take an examination for his enlistment in the United States Navy on Jan. 8, but he failed to meet requirements and rejoined the team.

With Carpenter getting healthy just about conference time and the return of Adams, the Razorbacks went on to post a 10-2 mark to tie Rice for top honors in the league loop.

All-Conference choice R.C. Pitts was the team's only All-SWC selection as well as serving of captain of a team that surprised many.

TURNING DOWN A BID At the conclusion of the regular season, Rose made the following statement regarding whether Arkansas or Rice, which had topped the Razorbacks 51-38 in their only meeting, should represent the SWC in the NCAA Tournament.

"Dean J.S. Watterman, president of the Southwest Athletic Conference, has advised me that there is no provision in the conference rules requiring a playoff in event there is a tie for the championship.

"The Arkansas basketball team has suffered numerous injuries due to both injuries and enlistment in the Army.

7. What Razorback duo earned All-American honors in 1929?

8. What 1992 Olympic gold medalist was once a Razorback basketball player?

For this reason, I prefer to waive consideration of Arkansas as an entry in a playoff to represent the district in the NCAA games at Kansas City. I hope that the NCAA committee for this district of the NCAA selects Rice Institute to represent the Southwest Conference.

"That school at this time can better uphold the basketball prestige of the Southwest Conference than our team in its present condition."

THE GENE LAMBERT ERA

With Lieutenant Glen Rose called to lead the Camp Grant football squad, Athletic Director and former Razorback All-American Dr. Gene Lambert took over the basketball team in 1942.

Four lettermen — 6-foot-7 senior captain Gordon Carpenter, guard Clayton Wynne and forwards A.B. Bradley and Jesse "Red" Wilson — were back and big things were expected from Ben Jones, who was a standout on the freshman squad a season earlier.

The Razorbacks jumped to a 10-0 start, including three wins in the All-College tournament at Oklahoma City. One of those tournament wins was a 66-44 pummeling of Texas, in which Wynne pumped in 24 points.

TCU took the All-College tournament championship and handed Arkansas its first loss of the season by whipping the Razorbacks, 37-25, before a crowd of 3,500 at Municipal Auditorium.

That loss seemed to take some of the steam out of the Razorbacks, who would go on to a 19-7 record and an 8-4 third-place finish in the SWC loop when they won just nine of their final 16 games.

Former Razorback All-American Gene Lambert took over for Rose when he was called to duty.

The 1943-44 squad gave Lambert his first SWC crown as a coach.

1943-44: TAKING BACK WHAT'S OURS

Having won 10 of the first 20 SWC titles, the Razorbacks kind of felt like any time they didn't win the league title that someone else was just holding the crown for them.

That's was the philosophy of the 1943-44 team, which set an SWC scoring mark, even though the squad was tabbed "dreary" in preseason predictions and returned only 6-foot-4 Ben Jones from the starting lineup of a year ago.

A squad that featured a quick guard in Deno Nichols, who would go on to led the conference in scoring, and a sharpshooting Baptist preacher named Bill "Preacher" Flynt confounded the experts.

Both Nichols and Flynt were tabbed two of the SWC's best five at the conclusion of Arkansas' 16-8 campaign. But the key in that mediocre overall record was the sparkling 11-1 record in league action, which gave the Razorbacks their 11th SWC championship.

Arkansas won five of its first six SWC games, with Flynt and Nichols leading the way.

Flynt had 21 points and Jones 19 when Arkansas routed SMU, 74-49, on Jan. 23, a game in which the Porkers came just a bucket shy of setting a new league

The 1943-44 non-conference season was spiced by a trip to New York City, where Jones scored a game-high 16 points and Nichols added 10 as the Razorbacks topped City College, 39-37, before a crowd of 17,000.

Arkansas ripped off five wins in its first six SWC games in '43-44, including a 60-29 win over TCU that saw Bill Flynt (shown here) pop in a season-high 29 points, just seven shy of former Arkansas standout John Adams' SWC mark.

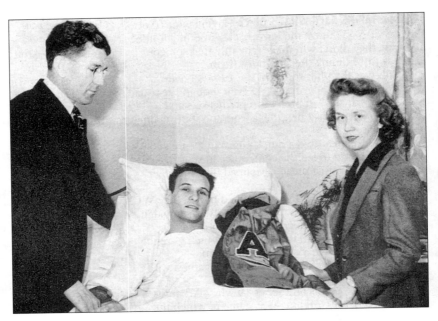

Coach Lambert presents a letter to Deno Nichols as wife Virginia watches.

mark for points in a single SWC game.

The Razorbacks took a break midway through the conference season to face Oklahoma A&M and its 7-0 center Bob Kurland in a two-game series in Oklahoma City.

Arkansas practiced for the game with one of its players standing inside the lane with a broom held up and Lambert worked the refs all week about Kurland's goaltending shots,

Kurland set a new school scoring record with 28 points in a easy 66-41 win over the Razorbacks.

Lambert changed strategies the next night and it almost worked. Arkansas played "keep-away" and held Kurland to 11 points in a 17-15 OSU win, in which the Razorbacks trailed just 11-10 at halftime.

As the Razorbacks were waiting to participate in the NCAA Tournament in Kansas City, a gift from the gods arrived in the form of 6-foot-10, 195-pound George Kok.

Kok had played two years of high school basketball in Michigan and some independent games, but was an unknown to Lambert when he enrolled as a freshman on March 4, 1944.

Kok joined the squad and traveled with the team for a practice game with the Camp Chaffee Tankers in Fort Smith as they waited for the NCAA tournament to start.

Because of some tragic circumstances, the scrimmage would be the only game Kok would play in that season.

A TRAGIC RIDE HOME The Razorbacks' season came to a chilling end when Nichols and Jones were both injured and team aide Everett Norris killed in a car wreck at midnight Saturday on Highway 71 on the way home from the game in Fort Smith.

They were in a station wagon along with Kok, Mike Schumchyk and Earl Wheeler and had stopped on the side of the road to repair a flat. The flat had been repaired and the squad was preparing to return home.

But a car driven by Washington County coroner Maurice Russell came over a rise in the road and trapped three men between the two cars.

Jones was also injured in the tragic accident.

Norris suffered severe lacerations, a crushed leg and other injuries, although newspaper reports indicated that extreme shock was the cause of his death at 4:30 a.m.

Nichols, who had just been named the head football and basketball coach at North Little High School, suffered a badly broken leg in two places while Jones had both of his legs broken.

The Razorbacks immediately canceled plans to play in the NCAA Tournament, an event won by the team that subbed for the Razorbacks, Utah.

Jones had to be transferred to Little Rock for an operation at Baptist Hospital while Nichols found himself needing blood transfusions to stay alive in a Fayetteville hospital.

One injury Nichols suffered that wasn't immediately discovered was actually credited with helping to save his life. That was a four-inch gash, which developed gas gangrene, a condition that is usually fatal within 48 hours.

But a Little Rock surgeon brought to Fayetteville in a State Police car found that the poison was actually working out of the four-inch wound instead of circulating over his entire body.

ANOTHER RECORD SETTING CREW With Kok beginning to develop and Flynt, who had quit school, rejoining the squad, the Razorbacks generated offensive fireworks not seen at the school before.

9. How did Arkansas do in its first few meetings with former head coach Francis Schmidt?

They averaged 58.4 per game in 1944-45, the highest average ever for an Arkansas team.

The Razorbacks performed even better while finishing second in the SWC race with a 9-3 mark by running up an average of 65.7 points per outing.

That included trashing the previous SWC single-game scoring record in a 94-28 humbling of Baylor, a night before whipping the Bears, 90-30.

Arkansas also rolled up big numbers on Texas A&M in 80-21 and 87-36 wins, but a loss at Texas and two at league champion Rice cost the team any chance at the title.

It was the first of three All-SWC campaigns for Kok,

Alvin Williams spent a great deal of his 1946-47 season on the free throw line where he set new SWC records for free throws made in a game and a season.

whose team came up short in two of three meetings with the 7-foot Kurland and national power Oklahoma State.

The Razorbacks, who were invited to the NCAA Tournament in Kansas City, downed Oregon, 79-76, before falling to Oklahoma State, 68-41, in the next round.

A STAR IS BORN The 6-foot-6 Alvin Williams, who was 24 years old at the time, wasted little time in establishing himself at Arkansas after transferring from Springfield Teachers College before the 1946-47 season.

He played a key role in the Razorbacks' wins over Nebraska and Kansas State in the Big Six tournament, an event in which they finished second after Kansas State downed them 56-41 in the championship game.

Williams used a penetrating style during the campaign to not only lead the conference in scoring at 17.1 per game, but to set a new SWC free throw record by making a whopping 76 during the season.

Perhaps his finest moment came during a 29-point effort in a 54-39 win over TCU, in which he set another league mark by connecting on 13 charity tosses in a single game.

He would join Kok, who was the SWC's second-leading scorer at 16 points per outing to form a potent offensive duo, and was the leading vote-getter on the All-SWC list.

The team finished the '46-47 season at 14-10 overall and 8-4 in the SWC, good enough for a tie for second behind 12-0 Texas.

1945-46: MEDIA FRIENDLY RAZORBACKS

Sportswriters around the state got to know the Arkansas basketball program this season better than any other because of a new publication from the athletic department.

It was manila folder with the words "U. Of Ark. Basketball 1945-46" and was filled with information on the upcoming season and players as well as the history of the program.

Arkansas' season would add a chapter that saw them go 16-7 overall and finish 9-3 and runner-ups in the SWC race.

Kok would earn his second All-SWC nod and showed both his skill and fiestiness in a 76-35 pounding of Camp Chaffee when he scored 13 points before being ejected.

THE GRAND RAPIDS WONDER
A highlight of the conference season were a couple of wins over Texas in which Kok pumped in a combined 43 points and high praise from Lambert.

Lambert insisted "The Grand Rapids Wonder," who was averaging a nation's best 20.3 points at the time, would be the best player in the United States.

"He will rank among the greatest basketball players in Southwest Conference history by the time his eligibility expires in 1948," Lambert boasted. "Big George is steadily improving. Contributing to his improvement is his recently acquired ability to use either his right hand or his left hand in making shots."

Kok scored a career-high 32 points in a 62-45 win over visiting Rice before a soldout Razorback crowd of 3,200 less than two weeks after Lambert's declaration.

George Kok would go on to score 1,644 points in his all-star career.

WHAT ABOUT KOK?
Despite being the league's second best point-producer, Kok was not named to the All-SWC first team after the 1946-47 season for the only time in his career.

SMU's Tommy Tomlinson got the nod and what made it even more strange was that Kok was named to *The Sporting News'* second-team All-America squad.

This was incredulous to Razorbacks fans, who knew Kok had a chance to become the first ever player to be All-SWC four years.

"Perhaps there were more proficent all-around performers, but it is difficult to rule out a man's value to his team and his scoring total when it comes to lining up against all the boys," proclaimed an editorial in the *Northwest Arkansas Times.* "Those who watched Kok play his heart out to help keep his team in the running are particular disappointed."

KOK's LAST STAND
The Razorbacks three seniors — George Kok, Alvin Williams and Tony Byles — led Arkansas to a 16-8 season and an 8-4 mark that was good enough for third in the SWC in 1947-48.

Kok was the leading scorer in the conference again and shook off a nagging ankle injury to post 33 points in a 66-63 overtime win over Baylor in his final college game.

His school record of 1,644 career points would stand for 30 years.

During the middle of the conference season of '47-48, Arkansas stopped off in Jonesboro to play Arkansas State after whipping Alabama. The 76-59 UA win would be the final meeting between the schools in 40 years. The two teams didn't meet again until an NIT matchup in 1987. Between those two games Arkansas adopted a policy of not playing in-state schools.

THE BI-COASTAL RAZORBACKS
Now traveling via the plane, the Razorbacks headed both East and West to show off their basketball ability.

Arkansas lost two games in New York City to New York University and LaSalle (Pa.), but fared much better on a trip to California.

Kok, who would not be denied as the best player in the league this season, was brilliant as the Razorbacks won three of their five games in tournaments in Los Angeles and San Francisco. He had 31 points in a 70-44 win to Pepperdine in the consolation finals of the first tournament.

1948-49: THREE WORTHY TEAMS Senior Ken Kearnes had long been a capable player, both in the two years before he quit school and in his junior season after returning from the layoff.

He was overshadowed by older players like Kok and Williams, but came into his own his senior season when he was named to the All-SWC squad and led his team to a share of the conference title and into the NCAA Tournament.

He poured in 17 points in a 54-50 win over defending champion Texas to push the Razorbacks into the SWC lead and had 11 points in his final regular season game, a 61-46 win over Texas A&M that secured a split of the title with Rice and Baylor.

There had never been a three-way tie for the SWC title and the NCAA decided to have a playoff in Dallas to decide who would be Southwest representative in the NCAA tourney in Kansas City.

Arizona was invited to play in the tournament as well, which was a financial bath for all the teams because of low attendance.

Arkansas, which had lost twice to Rice during the season, blew out the Owls, 50-34, behind Kearnes' 15 points that was even more impressive when you consider Razorback center Bob Ambler was tossed out four minutes into the game after throwing a punch.

Arizona shocked Baylor in the other semifinal, but the Wildcats were no match for Arkansas in the final as the Razorbacks rolled, 65-44.

Oregon State ended Arkansas' run however with a 56-38 whipping in the opening round of the NCAA Western Regional. The Razorbacks did outclass Wyoming in the consolation game, 61-48, in what would prove to be Lambert's last game at the helm.

THE PRESLEY ASKEW ERA

Presley Askew had long been a successful high school coach in Oklahoma and Arkansas before taking over as the Razorback freshman coach in 1948-49 and the head coaching reins of the varsity a season later.

The Arkansas media guide described him as "a student of the so-called control ball school" and "a molder of great basketball teams in the state of Arkansas."

RAZORBACK QUIZ

10. What is the highest scoring Arkansas team of all-time?

THE FRESHMAN FLAP

One of most interesting sidelights to 1949-50 season that carried itself in the following season was a flap that developed when five members of coach Ralph Ward's Arkansas freshman team played in an AAU tournament in Fayetteville in late February.

The five were seven-footer Billy "Toar" Hester, Fayetteville's Tryon Lewis, Pine Bluff's Joel Lucke and former Louisiana prep stars Wilburn Wood and Gerald Bryant.

SWC executive secretary James Stewart said the five would have to lose a year of varsity eligibility because of Section Two, Article 15 of the SWC regulations:

"Freshman teams shall not participate in meets of the A.A.U. or in any other open meets as representatives of their institution, but freshman athletes may participate in such meets as individuals without financial assistance from their institutions."

UA Athletic Director John Barnhill said at the time he believed things could be "worked out" when matters were taken up by the conference.

Indeed the SWC governing board decided later on to not penalize the players. The board did penalize the school, however, by preventing the Razorback team from working out the first 15 days of practice.

"No miracle man by any means, Askew's accomplishments on the hardwood can be contributed to hours of hard work, stressing fundamentals and teamwork," a bio in the media guide asserted. "He wants individual aggressiveness but far more — strives for cool, methodical teamwork that catches an opponent off guard, even if for a split-second."

He came to Fayetteville from Van Buren High School where he had taken four of his five Pointer teams to the state playoffs and watched his last three teams win all 30 of its conference games,

His all-time record was 300-112, with 12 tournament championships and seven conference titles.

Askew's first team — minus graduated starters Ken Kearnes, Clifford Horton and Johnny Campbell — had the challenge of facing the most ambitious schedule in school history and playing an incredible 18 of its 24 games away from home.

The first five Arkansas coaches all won conference titles.

FIVE COACHES, FIVE WINNERS With All-SWC selection Jimmy Cathcart, senior sub-captain Gerald Hudspeth, center Bob Ambler and Jack Hess leading the way, Arkansas turned it up a notch once league action rolled around.

The result was an 8-4 SWC mark, which was good enough for a share of the league crown with Baylor. The Razorbacks, who finished the season 12-12, closed with a rush by winning five of their last six games.

Arkansas grabbed its share of the crown with a 45-39 road win over TCU at the same time Baylor was downing SMU, 70-61, to create the deadlock.

The win meant Askew, the fifth coach in the school's history, kept alive a the streak of every Arkansas basketball coach having an SWC title on his resume.

It also was the Razorbacks' 13th SWC championship team in their 27-year run in the league, including nine outright titles. That was eight more than any other SWC member since 1923.

TRYING TO STAY FOCUSED Faced with 15 fewer practice days than the rest of the league, Askew took the unusual stance of closing practice during the preseason.

"We've lost 15 days to the other schools," Askew said, "and from here in we have to work at top speed. I cannot risk wasting any time and for that reason I am asking the public to bear with me during this training period in order that the team be as well prepared for for the coming schedule as possible. Every five minutes is going to help us this fall."

Hester was such a prodigous scorer in freshman games — he averaged 22 points in 12 games — that he was tagged as an All-American prospect by one national magazine.

He joined 6-foot-8 senior center Ambler, who he would split time with, and 6-6 sophomore Walter Kearnes to give the Razorbacks three strong players on its front line.

A SURPRISE OPENER The Southwest Conference granted all of its members a 25th game in 1950-51 with the proceeds to go to the Olympic Committee for the financing of the American entry in the annual Pan-American basketball tournament the following season.

The two-time defending SWC champion Razorbacks scheduled their game with Arkansas Tech, who took the two-hour trip up the mountain to test their 1950-51 unit and brought along former Fayetteville High standout Gene Wallick.

Arkansas led the game 30-20 at half, but found itself just up 43-40 midway through the second half.

At that point, guards D.L. Miller, Jack Hess and Gene Lambert played catch at midcourt for over seven minutes as Tech stayed back in its zone defense and refused to chase the ball.

Eventually the vistors began to foul and Kearnes broke loose for a layup on an out-of-bounds play as the Razorbacks went on to a 50-45 victory.

A DISAPPOINTING CAMPAIGN
Arkansas finished the season 13-11 overall, 7-5 in league contests.

The Razorbacks did at least finish the season off on a postive note with Hester pouring in 22 points in 22 minutes of action in the win over Rice to give him a team-high 204 points on the season.

1951-52: THE FIRST LOSING SEASON
Little could anyone envision when Arkansas jumped to a 13-0 lead in its season-opener against Central (Mo.) College that it would end up being the first squad in school history to post a losing campaign.

Despite having a school-record eight players taller than 6-foot-4, the Razorbacks struggled to a 10-14 mark that included just four wins in 12 SWC battles.

This also marked the first of five straight seasons that an Arkansas player failed to appear on the All-SWC team.

Presley Askew was not happy with having to play a preseason game with Arkansas Tech, but he was overruled by higher-ups.

Askew (center) talks strategy with Gene Lambert, Jr. (left) and Sammy Smith.

RAZORBACK QUIZ

11. What player led the Razorbacks in scoring in 1986-87 with the lowest average since 1961?

HESTER GOES HOME Even though he was having a solid season in which he was the SWC's second-leading scorer, Billy "Toar" Hester decided he was ready to pack it in Jan. 2, 1952.

Askew announced that Hester's reasons for quitting were that he was dissatisfied with both his own play and with school life and described the young man feelings as "an intense dislike" for school and a concurrent lack of enthusiasm for basketball.

Askew told the media that Hester had said no other school was involved, but that seemingly changed 10 days later when he enrolled at Centenary according to the Jan. 15, 1952, *Northwest Arkansas Times.*

"Centenary College of Shreveport announced yesterday that Hester will enroll there Wednesday. He will become eligible for competition in the Gulf States Conference next fall after completing 24 semester hours."

ASKEW STEPS DOWN The losing season wore on Arkansas' fans and four games before it was over, Askew announced he was stepping down in a letter of resignation on Jan. 16, 1952.

In the letter, Askew said he was stepping aside for "the best interests of the university, and the basketball program in particular."

Northwest Arkansas Times sports editor Alan Gilbert Jr. noted that those around the league were appalled at how the Razorback fans had all but forced Askew to step down because of lack of support.

Askew did go out a winner when Arkansas' Tryon Lewis swished a 40-footer at the buzzer to down Texas, 45-44, in Fayetteville.

RAZORBACK QUIZ

12. Arkansas owns what record because of its 120-101 win over Loyola Marymount in 1989?

A BLACK EYE One other thing that put a black eye on the 1952-53 season was the allegation that the 1950 Arkansas-Kentucky game in Little Rock might have been fixed.

Heavily favored Kentucky, the defending national champion, edged Arkansas, 57-53. The Razorbacks won the SWC that season, but were just 12-12 overall.

New York district attorney Frank Hogan, who broke the college basketball point-shaving scandal the previous year, finally got Kentucky's Walter Hirsch to testify as a material witness.

This followed Kentucky's stance to not allow Hirsch to enroll in school unless he would testify about alleged allegations that Hirsch, Barnstable and James Line accepted bribes to shave points in games played in Kentucky and Arkansas in 1949-50.

An affidavit charged that Hirsch, Barnstable and Line — now working for an Arkansas oil company — accepted $500 each to fix the Kentucky-DePaul game and $1,000 each to fix the Arkansas-Kentucky game.

The affidavit said that the trio turned down $7,500 to fix an NIT tournament game with City College and $1,000 to fix a Kentucky-St. John's at the behest of fixers Eli Kaye and Nicholas Englists.

THE SECOND GLEN ROSE ERA

His nickname may have been "Gloomy Glen" but everyone around the University of Arkansas athletic department was all smiles after talking former player and coach Glen Rose into returning as head basketball coach.

A cartoon in the *Northwest Arkansas Times* on March 15, 1952, featured a Razorback with bandages — symbolizing the downtrodden Arkansas basketball program — shaking hands with Rose.

Rose, who signed a five-year deal worth $7,000 a year, had been highly successful during his first stint (1933-42) as the Razorback boss. His teams won five SWC titles in nine years before he entered the military service.

Rose returned to Fayetteville and was the Razorback football coach for two years before becoming business manager for athletics. He had accepted the head basketball post at Stephen F. Austin in 1946.

The campus rejoiced when Rose agreed to leave Stephen F. Austin and return to coach at Arkansas.

THE RUNNIN' RAZORBACKS Rose wasted little time in replacing Askew's ball-control offense with his fast-break attack, one that was installed during the 18-day spring practice that was allowed back then.

Arkansas averaged 70 points per game in a 13-game spring scrimmage format and upped the tempo even more when the 1952-53 season rolled around.

Although the Razorbacks lost their season-opener to Clarence Iba-led Tulsa, 69-50, they opened their home campaign in grand style with a school-record 102-71 win over Mississippi State.

Gene Lambert and Orval Elkins poured in 20 points each in the win, which broke the school record set in a 101-37 thrashing of Sedalia, Mo., back in 1945-46.

The new mark lasted exactly two games as Lambert scored 27 points and Manuel Whitley 20 in a 104-72 thumping of Ole Miss in Little Rock.

THE SWC MIDSEASON TOURNAMENT The first SWC midseason tournament was such a success that the league decided to make it a tradition that would last for nine years.

The first two preseason events were held at the State Fairgrounds in Texas in conjunction with the Cotton Bowl before moving on to Houston for the final seven years.

Sporting a 3-1 record and putting up points like no

RAZORBACK QUIZ

13. What is the highest scoring Southwest Conference game in Arkansas history?

Joe Telford (25) moves into position in Arkansas' 49-47 win over Baylor in 1953.

league team before, Arkansas was dubbed the tourney favorite in 1952 and the Razorbacks looked the part while blasting non-league invitee Arizona, 68-51, in their opener.

But a horrible 16-of-31 performance from the foul line in the semifinal spelled doom for Arkansas as SMU pulled off a 65-61 upset.

The Razorbacks did grab third in an event they never won by downing Baylor, 59-54.

ANOTHER YEAR IN THE BASEMENT Although Arkansas was 5-2 at one point in its non-conference slate, things went downhill once the Razorbacks opened the SWC race.

Opening losses at Texas A&M and Texas were the beginning of a second consecutive 4-8 SWC campaign that would find Arkansas at the bottom of the league standings for a second straight year.

Arkansas went into its season finale against visiting and current cellar dweller SMU with a chance to avoid having the school's first losing season ever.

But despite Whitley's 27 points and Floyd Sagely's 15, SMU routed the homestanding Razorbacks, 74-49, to leave Arkansas 10-11 for the season.

It was the final game in the careers of both Walter

RAZORBACK QUIZ

14. How many field goal attempts did Dean Tolson take when setting the school mark in 1974?

Kearns, who was named second-team All-SWC, and Gene Lambert Jr., the team's leading scorer with 270 points.

REBUILDING PROJECT In addition to trying to fight off the stigma of two straight cellar-dwelling seasons, Rose found himself facing the challenge of replacing exactly 50 percent of his offense in 1953-54.

Manuel Whitley was drafted and was no longer available along with graduated standouts Lambert and Walter Kearns. This trio had combined to score 668 points in 1952-53.

Rose looked to two returning starters — Orval Elkins and Floyd Sagely — to carry the load and would also get big boosts from sophomores Gerald Barnett of Harrison and Buddy Smith, Raymond Shaw, Norman Smith, Carroll Scroggins and Marvin Adams.

STORMIN' NORMAN Sagely, a football star, got into the lineup in time for Arkansas' game with visiting Missouri on Dec. 20, 1953, and quickly played a vital role in his team's success.

In a game that had 15 ties, Sagely connected on his first basket of the season when he drove the lane with 20 seconds left to put Arkansas up, 66-64.

On the ensuing trip down court, Sagely and Missouri player Norm Stewart — who would go on to become MU's legendary coach and face Arkansas many times — got tangled up and batted the ball out of bounds. The referee called for a jump ball with five seconds left.

That tap went out of bounds as did 6-foot-8 Missouri center Bob Reiter and Arkansas' Leo McDonald, forcing yet another jump ball with one second left.

Legendary Missouri coach Norm Stewart was involved in a key play in Arkansas' 65-64 win over the Tigers in 1953-54.

Off that tip, McDonald fouled Reiter and the Mizzou center was given a chance to tie the contest.

"A tremendous cry arose from the fans standing in anticipation of the official verdict and Reiter made his first free throw against a solid background of boos and whistles," noted a game report in the *Northwest Arkansas Times*. "He missed (the second throw) and that was that."

TRYING ANYTHING Rose changed his lineup almost every game as more than 11 players earned starting berths early on in the SWC season.

Arkansas couldn't really get anything going because of what Rose dubbed "lack of offense from a post player and excessive fouling."

The Razorbacks found themselves virtually eliminated from the chase early on when they dropped three of their first four conference games, including a humbling 80-55 home loss at the hands of the Rice Owls.

If that wasn't enough, defensive star Don Trumbo

Floyd Sagely, a football and basketball standout for the Razorbacks, accepts a trophy in 1954.

announced he was leaving school and joining the Marines after the jolting loss.

Arkansas (13-9, 6-6) did regroup enough in midseason to post a winning record, but missed a chance to finish above .500 in league play when Texas dropped the Razorbacks, 67-57, at Fayetteville in the season finale.

BABY STEPS Arkansas continued to inch its way back up the SWC ladder in 1954-55 as Rose took a team that returned only five lettermen and molded it into a competitive unit by the end of the season.

The Razorbacks (14-9 overall, 8-4 SWC) closed with a rush in league action by winning eight of their last 10 games to notch a tie for second.

Rose had veterans Norman and Buddy Smith, Barnett and Carroll Scroggins on hand and got big lifts in the form of 6-foot-4, 210-pound junior college Pete Butler and sophomore Terry Day.

Butler's biggest outing of the year was a 31-point performance in a 79-74 win over Texas late in the season. That made him only the third Razorback in history — John Adams and George Kok were the others — to top the 30-point barrier.

That win put Arkansas in a second-place tie with SMU, just a game back of league-leading TCU's 8-3 mark and the two combatants met in the next contest in Fayetteville.

Jim Krebs, SMU's 6-foot-8 center, went wild and scored 30 points as the Mustangs eliminated the Razorbacks from the conference race with an 83-69 win in Dallas.

1955-56: A HORRIBLE START Rose did have four players returning who had scored more than 200 points the previous campaign — Jerald Barnett, Buddy Smith, Pete Butler and Terry Day — and got a boost with the return of former standout Manuel Whitley after a two-year Army stint.

He also had the chance for some positive energy from the move into Razorback Fieldhouse, which would later be named in honor of athletic director John Barnhill.

But there was no lift from the new facility as Arkansas started the season 0-6, including it's first two games at Razorback Fieldhouse. The Razorbacks also dropped a exhibition game to the Phillips 66 Oilers during this start, which was the worst in the school's 32-year basketball history.

AN INAUSPICIOUS BEGINNING To say that the first-ever game at the new venue was disappointing would be a major understatement.

Not only did Southeastern Oklahoma State edge the Razorbacks, 65-64, but fans were less than comfortable throughout the contest because the heating units in the building failed to work.

If that wasn't bad enough, cables supporting the new scoreboard gave way and the new expensive piece of equipment crashed to the floor and was inoperable for

Norman Smith was named to the second team All-SWC after the 1954-55 season.

The Razorbacks set four SWC marks in a 110-89 throttling of TCU on March 1, 1955, in Fayetteville. Arkansas set school and SWC records for most points in a game; most free throws made (46) and attempted (65) and joined with TCU to set a mark for most combined free throws (107) in a single league contest.

What was then known as Arkansas Fieldhouse when it opened in 1955 is now Barnhill Arena.

the game.

Instead officials had to keep time with a stopwatch and the score was announced frequently over a portable loudspeaker.

RIGHTING THE SHIP The Razorbacks ended their futility in a big way and got their first win of the 1955-56 season with a 80-49 thumping of Texas A&M in their final game in the SWC's late December tournament.

Whitley, who was named all-tournament, had 20 points in the win and 72 in the three-day event.

Norm Stewart had 14 points as heavily favored Missouri edged Arkansas, 51-50, in the next game, which dropped the Razorbacks to 1-8 but also showed how far the team had progressed.

Arkansas took its newly-found momentum and turned it into a 5-0 league start during a span in which it also picked up a non-conference win over Ole Miss in Memphis.

Having lost their first four outings in their new building, the Razorbacks finally found victory in their new surroundings by pounding Rice, 84-70, in a game that also served as the dedication of the new arena.

John Barnhill was honored when Razorback Fieldhouse changed to Barnhill Fieldhouse in 1957.

FANS COME ALIVE A bonus for Arkansas was the fact that former defensive star Don Trumbo returned to the team in early February of 1956 after a stint with the Marines. Trumbo, a 6-3 forward, had averaged 21.6 points, for his service team.

Trumbo got back just in time for the Razorbacks' big showdown of conference unbeatens with SMU, a game which drew a sellout crowd of 6,000.

SMU took control of the race with a 58-53 win in which Arkansas shot a meager 24.7 percent from the field.

The league-leading and unbeaten SMU squad ended all doubt who was the best team in the league by downing Arkansas, 80-72, on Feb. 26, 1956.

The win, which was in the first Southwest Conference game carried live on television, boosted the Ponies to 11-0 and left Arkansas in second and mathematically eliminated with an 8-3 mark.

NOT THE SAME Arkansas scored 400 points more than its opponents and grabbed 200 more rebounds than its foes while going 11-12 for the second straight season, in 1956-57.

The Razorbacks finished just 5-7 in league action in a season that saw them plagued by inconsistent play.

Terry Day did become just the eighth Razorback to score more than 300 points in a single season with 301, an average of 12.5 points an outing.

1957-58: ROSE'S RUNTS With a roster that featured no one taller than 6-foot-6 in a league that had its share of big men, Rose had to somehow come up with an attack that would give his troops their best chance at victory.

He did just that by going to a double post — even without a giant to man either spot — and the result was

Rose was constantly trying to teach his teams the finer points of the game.

Don Trumbo helped spark the Razorbacks on his return from the Marines.

Terry Day became the eighth Razorback in school history to top 300 points in a single year.

RAZORBACK QUIZ

15. Name the top single-season scorer in Razorback history.

a glorious season that ended with the Razorbacks (17-10, 9-5) winning their first conference title since 1950 and playing in the NCAA Tournament.

ASKEW RETURNS The 1957-58 season brought the first SWC title since Presley Askew's inaugural season at the helm of the Razorbacks.

It was ironic that Askew, who resigned under pressure after three seasons, made an appearance back in Fayetteville during the season with his New Mexico State squad right after the Razorbacks lost their season-opener at Oklahoma.

New Mexico State led by as many as 11 points in the second half as "Arkansas started out the game with as much enthusiasm as a vegetarian sitting down to a plate of hamburger," reported the *Northwest Arkansas Times.* "New Mexico, running the old gang blocks and screens that Coach Presley Askew is so fond of, took advantage of Arkansas' lethargy."

The Razorbacks woke up in time to rip off a 12-1 spurt in just 3:45 to deadlock the game 40-40. Larry Grisham had 13 of his 26 points in the game's final 13 minutes as Arkansas pulled out a 59-50 victory in what was now Barnhill Fieldhouse.

A BALANCED RACE The 1957-58 SWC turned out to be as competitive from top to bottom as ever.

Those final two weeks proved quite entertaining for Razorbacks fans, who were watching All-SWC choice Fred Grim, a 6-0 guard, go on a scoring rampage.

The Razorbacks, who jumped out a 5-0 start, dropped to 7-4 with consecutive losses to Texas Tech, Texas A&M and Rice to fall into third place behind co-leaders SMU and Tech.

Texas A&M upset Texas Tech to leave the Mustangs in the driver's seat for their fourth straight league crown, but they couldn't seal the deal.

Arkansas regained a share of the lead as it pounded Baylor, 79-55, and A&M upset SMU, 43-42, on a last-second goaltending call.

That left Arkansas with just a home date with Texas

Larry Grisham starred on the Razorback's first SWC title team since 1950.

Wayne Dunn lettered in 1956, 1957 and 1958 for teams that went a combined 37-36.

standing between it and at least a share of the title.

Grim, who would score 380 points during the season and earn a berth on the All-SWC squad, led the way with 18 points as the Razorbacks downed the Longhorns, 74-60.

Those 18 points by Grim allowed him to set a new SWC scoring mark for Arkansas players with 235 points.

SMU's regular-season finale win over Baylor set up a one-game playoff in Shreveport between the Mustangs and the Razorbacks, who had split the two-game season series by winning close games on their own home court.

Before 9,130 fans in Shreveport, Grim tossed in 18 and Jay Carpenter 15 as Arkansas pulled out a 61-55 victory.

Eddie Sutton, who later coached Arkansas, hurt the Razorbacks as an Oklahoma State player in 1957-58.

EDDIE, WILT AND THE BIG O Arkansas opened the NCAA Tournament in Kansas City against a familiar nemesis in Oklahoma State (formerly Oklahoma A&M), who had whipped the Razorbacks 16 straight times.

Little did Razorback fans know at the time that this would be their last visit to the NCAA Tournament for 19 years until one of the current OSU stars took over as coach in Fayetteville.

That standout was Eddie Sutton, who poured in 28 points as OSU downed Arkansas, 65-40.

Kansas State defeated Cincinnati, 83-80, in the night's first game despite 30 points from Oscar Robertson, whose game was taken in by University of Kansas star Wilt Chamberlin.

The pair were generally regarded as the best two players in the country that season.

Robertson, averaging 34.5 points per game, showed just how many plays and points he could make the following night when he bombed in an NCAA-record 56 points as Cincinnati thrashed Arkansas, 97-62.

At one point Robertson had outscored the Razorbacks 43-42 and pumped in his final two points to tie Arkansas, 56-56.

Emerson's Pat Foster was a All-SWC player at Arkansas and later a trusted Sutton coaching aide.

STARTING OVER AGAIN There were some promising sophomores on board in 1958-59, including future Razorback assistant coach Pat Foster of Emerson, Ronnie Garner and Hot Springs' Clyde Rhoden, who would go on to become a two-time All-SWC selection.

Arkansas suffered through a 9-14 season, including a 6-8 mark in SWC action, but there were a few bright spots.

One of those was a 61-57 win over Texas Tech in the SWC-opener, which doubled as the first ever televised game from Fayetteville. The telecast reached 30 stations in six states.

Another was a sophomore-highlighted 77-74 win

over Texas, the Razorbacks' 10th straight win over the Longhorns since 1955. Rhoden poured in 29 points and Garner 21.

Texas Tech whipped Arkansas, 80-69, in Fayetteville in the season finale in a game in which Garner had a season-high 24 points and future Red Raider head coach Gerald Myers led his team with 20.

BREAKING THE OSU JINX
Arkansas' fab sophomore trio of Foster, Rhoden and Garner brought back plenty of firepower for 1959-60, but the Razorbacks' toughest chore was going to be finding some rebounders to replace the graduated Carpenter and Thompson.

That problem was evident in Arkansas' season-opening 75-71 loss to visiting Missouri, but nowhere to be found in the second game of the season against an old rival.

Foster led the way with 12 points as the Razorbacks topped Oklahoma State, 54-50, in the school's first win over OSU in 16 games. It was the first win for Arkansas in the series since the 1944-45 season.

Using his patented off-the-shoulder jumper, All-SWC pick Rhoden averaged 16.2 points during a season that would find Arkansas finishing 12-11 overall and 7-7 and in a tie for fourth in the SWC race.

Rhoden tied his career-high with the third 29-point game of his Razorback career, all coming in overtime wins. This season's outburst came in a 90-83 double overtime win at Baylor.

Rhoden broke Grim's record for points by an Arkansas player in SWC play with 258 and also set a new SWC record for free throws made in a season with 86.

A VETERAN CREW
Rose returned his entire starting lineup in 1960-61 and welcomed hotshot sophomore Tommy Boyer, who averaged 20.4 points per game on the freshman team.

"We had our best shooting team in years last season, but we still finished 7-7 in the conference," Rose said. "I don't know that we will improve on our scoring so any real improvement in our standing will have to come somewhere else and that's where I'm worried. We just don't have good speed and that's bound to hurt."

Both Foster and Rhoden were consistent through their senior campaigns that ended with nabbing two of the five spots on the All-SWC squad.

Foster, with a high of 29 points in an 88-74 win over TCU, averaged a team-leading 15.4 points per game and was even better in league action by scoring at a 17.9 clip.

Rhoden averaged just 11.4 overall, but stepped it up during a league race that saw him pour in 13.4 per game.

Texas Tech would capture the SWC title with a 11-3

Garner formed a high-scoring trio with Foster and Rhoden.

Clyde Rhoden was a two-time All-SWC choice.

Carlton was one of five players on the 1960-61 team who averaged double figures in scoring.

Foster (12) averaged a team-leading 15.4 points per game during the 1960-61 season.

mark, which came courtesy of a offensive explosion that put up a league-record 1,102 points during the season.

Arkansas (16-7) ended up third with a 9-5 mark.

1961-62: THE BEST START EVER

For all the tradition and success that surrounded the Arkansas basketball program, there has never been a better start in school history than the one Rose's 1961-62 team put up.

After a season-opening 85-74 loss at Kansas in which they played a zone, the Razorbacks switched to a man-to-man defense and ripped off a school-record nine straight wins beginning with a 72-68 win over Missouri in their home-opener.

Carlton had 21 points, 6-foot-5 junior Larry Wofford 16 points and 15 rebounds and Boyer — wearing a facemask because of a broken nose — had 15 points against Missouri.

The surge included an 84-81 overtime road win over LSU in Shreveport in which Carlton netted 24 points.

Larry Wofford had 16 points and 15 rebounds in a win over Missouri in 1961.

DEADEYE ACCURACY

It was not a good idea to put Arkansas at the free throw line during the season as the Razorbacks nailed a school-record 77.6 percent of their attempts.

It was especially unwise to foul All-SWC choice Carlton or Boyer, who took turns leading the nation in the marksmanship and finished 1-2.

Carlton couldn't miss early on and hit 55 of his first 58 charity tosses, a 94.7 clip. He ended up hitting an SWC-record 140 of 159 (88 percent) for the season.

Boyer ended up leading the nation by hitting 93.3 percent of his free throws (125 of 134), including 30 in a row at one point. He became the first college player to ever hit more than 90 percent.

In addition, Carlton became only the second player in school history to top 1,000 points in a career and Boyer set a new SWC season scoring mark for UA players with 269 points.

Boyer led the nation in free throw shooting at 93.3 percent in 1961-62.

CRASH AND BURN

A wide-open race was expected for the SWC in 1961-62, with Arkansas off to a hot start and several other teams looking capable of competing for the title.

Arkansas bounced the Aggies, 64-59, in its league opener, but then lost at Texas, 73-59, and at SMU, 77-70, and never seemed to recover.

After such a promising start, the Razorbacks lost nine of their final 14 games to finish 14-10 overall and just 5-9 in the SWC (sixth place).

ROSE'S 20th

Rose's troops celebrated the opening of the 1962-63 season — Rose's 20th season at the helm of the

Glen Rose shows his humorous side as former NBA announcer Joe Garagiola cracks up.

Jim Magness shined with 20 points and 14 rebounds in a win over Ole Miss in 1963-64.

Razorbacks — by edging Kansas in overtime at Barnhill Fieldhouse, 64-62.

Boyer sent the game into overtime with a turnaround 20-footer and hit another to put the Razorbacks up 61-60 and ahead for good in overtime.

Arkansas ended its non-conference slate 5-3, including a 72-70 loss to LSU at Little Rock, where Boyer exploded for a career-high 35 points.

The Razorbacks then got off to a good start in the SWC race by slipping past SMU, 73-71, at Dallas in its league opener, but never really put together a winning streak the rest of the season.

Arkansas finished 13-11 overall, 8-6 and fourth in the SWC race, but did end its season on a winning note.

All-SWC selection Boyer left it all on the court in his final college game while pouring in 31 points in a 104-94 win over TCU in Barnhill.

He ended up with two NCAA records — the aforementioned free throw percentage mark and most consecutive free throws made (44).

Boyer also notched seven Arkansas records including most points in three SWC seasons (730), most points in an SWC season (307), SWC scoring average (21.9), free throws made in a full season (147), free throws made in an SWC season (113), free throws attempted in an SWC season (123) and field goals made in an SWC season (97).

A STAR IS BORN Former Fayetteville High star J.D. McConnell had been a solid contributor his sophomore year as the team's fifth-leading scorer, but saved his best game for the 1963-64 season finale.

McConnell had 23 points and 14 rebounds as the Razorbacks slapped hapless TCU around, 108-77, before a small crowd of 1,500 fans. The 108 points was two shy of the school record, but did set a new mark for offensive output at Barnhill Fieldhouse.

1964-65: IT'S FOOTBALL'S YEAR Unless it won a national championship, there was no way for the basketball team to upstage Frank Broyles' football team in 1964-65.

That's because the Razorback football team went 12-0 and was awarded the Grantland Rice national championship after a 10-7 Cotton Bowl win over Alabama capped its perfect season.

Broyles and his team were bitterly disappointed when unbeaten and untied Alabama was voted No. 1 in the final Associated Press poll, but overjoyed when Texas beat the Crimson Tide, 21-17, in the Orange Bowl.

"This is something I know the people of Arkansas have dreamed about for a long time," Broyles said. "I know that this has to be the proudest moment in the athletic history — for the players, the university and our fans."

When the basketball team lost its first three games, it was clear that the football team was not going to be upstaged.

J.D. McConnell had his coming out party in Arkansas' record-setting 108-77 win against TCU.

Glen Rose is regarded as one of the best tacticians to ever coach at Arkansas.

John Talkington had a game-winning shot one year and set a single-game rebound mark the following season.

Sugg (32) drives the lane in a season where he would set a single-game record with his 41 points against Centenary.

The Razorbacks turned in their second straight 9-14 season. They actually moved up a spot in the SWC standings while winning just five games, one less than they had captured the previous season.

1965-66: ROSE'S LAST STAND Little did anyone know going into the season that Glen Rose's 23rd year coaching the Razorbacks would also be his last. His retirement announcement was not made until the season was over.

His final season ended with a 13-10 mark, 7-7 in league action to bring his all-time Razorback coaching record to 325-201, the most wins of any coach in the school's history through 1995-96.

SUGG EXPLODES Junior Ricky Sugg, a 6-1 guard who was the leading returning scorer, was averaging just eight points through the first three games before putting on

the finest individual scoring performance ever in a 90-61
Arkansas win over Centenary on Dec. 13, 1965.

Sugg scored 22 points in the first half of a 41-point
performance that broke Johnny Adams' school mark of
36 points set a quarter of a century earlier.

Sugg hit 13 of 13 free throws in the win.

RAZORBACK QUIZ

16. How many 30-
point single game
efforts have there
been in UA history?

THE SWC RACE Arkansas opened the league race on the
road against a TCU team that was averaging 92 points,
but was giving up 100 a game in a 2-5 start.

The Razorbacks erased two 10-point deficits, but fell
88-85 at Daniel Meyer Coliseum for the first Horned
Frog win in the series in seven years.

Arkansas entered what would prove to be the final
game of Rose's coaching career with a 6-7 SWC mark
and a chance to send him out with a .500 mark.

It was also the final game for six Arkansas seniors,
who helped to pound Texas A&M, 94-71, before 4,500
fans with Talkington leading the way with 29 points.

ROSE CALLS IT QUITS Two days after the season was over,
Rose announced he would be retiring effective June 30
and that assistant P.T. "Duddy" Waller would be named
the new coach.

"It was not an easy decision, but I've just been
through too many overtimes and last-second games,"
Rose said. "I only have one set of nerves and they've been
under constant strain for too many years. I think it is
time to turn it over to a younger man and I know Coach
Waller will give it his full energy.

"I've been extremely fortunate to stay in this
profession as long as I have. Coaching has been very
good to me."

THE DUDDY WALLER ERA

After biding his time as a loyal assistant for nine years,
Duddy Waller finally got his chance to take over the
Razorbacks in 1966-67.

The 6-17 overall record and 4-10 record in league
play should not have come as much of a surprise since
the Razorbacks returned only three lettermen, none of
whom had ever started.

Ironically the first win of the season came over an
opponent that many of the school's best teams had
trouble recording a victory over — Oklahoma State.

The Razorbacks downed the homestanding Cowboys,
51-46, as senior Wally Freeman poured in 19 points and
senior Tommy Rowland had 14. Arkansas hit an
astounding (for then) 53 percent of its shots.

Rowland led the way during the Razorbacks' subpar

Waller's last team
posted an all-time
worst record of 5-19.

Duddy Waller was a solid recruiter as an assistant who finally got his chance as a head coach.

Rick Tanneberger put on one of the greatest shooting displays in school history, hitting 10 of 11 field goals and six of seven free throws.

season with an 18-point per game average while Freeman was second at 13.2.

1967-68: WALLER'S BEST JOB Waller had a four-year run at the helm of the Razorbacks and found his most success in the 1967-68 season. After starting out the previous season 1-6, the Razorbacks really stressed getting off to a better start.

They did just that by winning three of their first five games and, although the Razorbacks did slump in midseason, improving their SWC mark from 4-10 to 7-7 in one season.

The biggest win of the season was set up when Texas came into its season-finale with visiting Arkansas with a share of the SWC lead with TCU and Baylor.

The Razorbacks entered the game with a 9-14 overall mark and a 6-7 league record, but had downed the Longhorns in Little Rock, 85-80.

Arkansas' Jack Kimbrell proved to be the hero by hitting a tiebreaking free throw with 11 seconds left and then grabbing Kurt Papp's missed shot and tucking it away for the win.

BREAKING THE BARRIER The 1968-69 season might be remembered more than anything by the fact that Thomas Johnson of Menifee became the first African-American varsity basketball player at the University of Arkansas.

Johnson was the freshman team's third-leading scorer (15.5) in 1967-68 after a tremendous high school career in which he averaged 30.4 points per game his senior season.

1969-70: DUDDY'S LAST STAND

In a year that is more remembered for President Nixon's visit to Fayetteville for the "Game of the Century" between the Arkansas and Texas football teams, the pressure became too much for Waller to bear.

The Razorbacks posted the school's all-time worst record of 5-19, including a conference worst 3-11 that placed them in the cellar.

Waller, under intense pressure and criticism from the fans, announced on March 1 that he was stepping down.

"With everyone concerned, I felt it would be better if I just dropped out," Waller said. "I knew about all the criticism and I felt it would just be better if I turned them in."

The Razorbacks heard about Waller's decision and went out and whipped Texas, 78-61, in what was also the final home appearance for seniors Tanneberger,

A highlight of the 1968-69 season was the first-ever Little Rock Classic, which featured two divisions with four college teams and a high school field of 12. The two-day festival at Barton Coliseum had four games each day. The Razorbacks won the inaugural event and Gary Stephens was named outstanding college player of the tourney.

Tommy Rowland was the Razorbacks' leading point producer in 1967-68.

Robert McKenzie, James Eldridge and Danny Keeter.

McKenzie led the way with 23 points while super sophomore Almer Lee had 21. Tanneberger led the way on the boards with 12.

THE LANNY VAN EMAN ERA

Lanny Van Eman came to Arkansas after being a successful assistant under Ralph Miller at Iowa.

Lanny Van Eman, who had been assisting Ralph Miller at Iowa, beat out some 50 other applicants to nab the vacant Razorback coaching post in 1970.

Van Eman and the Hawkeyes were coming off a Big 10 championship and he was given a strong recommendation by Miller.

Van Eman, who raced right off to Hutchinson (Kan.) Junior College to recruit after his announcement as the new head coach, was glad to be in Fayetteville.

"I am delighted not only with becoming a head coach but also to work in an athletic program like the one they have at Arkansas," Van Eman said.

His four-year contract paid him $15,000 per year, $2,000 more than Waller was getting.

Van Eman added Jimmy Rogers, who would later go on to coach the Boston Celtics, and Tommy Matthews to his staff.

BIG NUMBERS, BIG LOSSES Van Eman saw himself facing the same losing problems his predecessor did although the defeats became much more entertaining at least, with his up-tempo, high-scoring unit.

Arkansas (5-21, 1-13) set records for worst overall and league finish in 1970-71 but did score more than 100 points four times. However, the Razorbacks won only two of those games as their defense allowed opponents to top the century mark five times.

The Razorbacks did match the school record for points in a 111-110 home loss to Baylor in the next-to-last game of the season and also set a new mark for most points allowed in a 115-100 loss to visiting Oklahoma.

The SWC season was less than kind to the Razorbacks, who dropped their first nine games and threw in a loss to Wabash (Kan.) for good measure.

The only SWC win the Razorbacks could garner that season was an 88-87 win at rival Texas.

AMAZING ALMER AND VERNON One of the chief beneficiaries of Van Eman's arrival was junior Almer Lee, who averaged a team-leading 19.2 points and was named the SWC's sophomore of the year after the 1970-71 season.

That included 20.6 points per game in league play, including a career-best 30 points in a loss to Texas A&M.

Another beneficiary was 6-6 power forward Vernon

17. What Walter Camp football All-American was declared ineligible prior to the school's first ever basketball game?

Almer Lee led the team in scoring during the 1970-71 season with a 19.2 average.

Murphy, who became the first Razorback to put together back-to-back 30-point games in a win over Missouri-St. Louis and a loss to Oklahoma.

He averaged 17.6 points for the year — with a 36-point performance in the 111-110 loss to Baylor — and a team-leading 8.9 rebounds.

THE UNDEFEATED SHOATS When 6-8 freshman Dean Tolson ripped off 40 points and 25 rebounds in the Arkansas freshman team's 109-76 win over Westark Junior College, the Razorbacks were off and running to an unbeaten 16-0 season in 1970-71.

While the varsity was struggling, the Shoats were rarely challenged and capped their perfect 16-0 season with a 114-106 win over Beebe Junior College.

"I'm just glad it's over," said Matthews, who guided the freshman. "This is a great thing for the University of Arkansas, but it is even greater for the players. They really worked hard for this."

Tolson averaged 30.4 points and 20.4 rebounds per game as a freshman.

A SMALL STEP AHEAD Although Arkansas ended up just 8-18 in 1971-72, the Razorbacks did continue to pack in the fans and actually got off to a decent start.

Rated as a potential SWC darkhorse in part because of

Dean Tolson was the key cog on a freshman team that went 16-0 in 1970-71.

Tolson's elevation to the varsity and junior college transfer Martin Terry's arrival, the Razorbacks opened by winning three of its first six games.

Junior College transfer John Campbell set a new single-game school record with 21 rebounds in a 102-72 win over Rockhurst in the season's fourth game.

Arkansas (8-18, 5-9) turned into a record-setting unit during the final two games of its campaign.

The Razorbacks wasted Baylor, 131-109, to obliterate the previous school mark of 110 as Tolson tossed in 34 points and Terry 33. The point total also set a new SWC mark.

Arkansas topped the century mark again in its final game, a 113-108 win at Rice that doubled as its first road win of the season. Terry led the way with 33 points and Tolson added 30.

TERRY'S EXPLOSIONS Terry was an offensive force throughout his All-SWC season in 1971-72, averaging 24.3 points per game and absolutely exploding in several games.

One of those was a school-record 46-point outburst in a 100-89 win over Texas A&M, five more points than Ricky Sugg's old mark of 41.

Martin Terry went on to earn his doctorate.

He also pumped in 40 against Southern Illinois, 34 against Texas, 33 against Baylor, 32 at Texas A&M and 31 at Rice and scored more than 20 points in 12 other games.

Terry, the Razorbacks' first All-SWC selection since 1963, scored more than 25 points in each of his last seven games his junior season and set 18 school records during the season.

1972-73: A BREAKTHROUGH

With Terry and Tolson back and former players Pat Foster and Bobby Vint on board as assistants, Arkansas had every right to be excited about a possible breakthrough in its basketball program.

That excitement was heightened by the addition of 6-foot-2 sophomore guard Ricky Medlock, whose 33.4 points per game average as a freshman set a school record and led the SWC conference.

One of Medlock's big games was a 57-point

Martin Terry was a high-scoring, two-time All-SWC selection who helped the Arkansas program get back on its feet.

performance against Poteau Junior College in which he hit 21 of 35 field goals.

A GREAT START A 5-1 start was the best opening for an Arkansas team since 1961-62 and was capped when the Razorbacks embarrassed Georgia State, 70-39.

"This team is finally buying our theory of defense and rebounding," Van Eman said. "We've outrebounded five of our six opponents. Since we're not a shooting team, we have to play good defense."

Arkansas was surprised in the opening round of its own Razorback Classic in December by Cornell, 78-77, despite 29 points from Terry, whose 27.8 average was eighth in the nation at the time.

Ricky Medlock once scored 57 points in a freshman game.

AN SWC CONTENDER Arkansas had been an SWC pretender since its last league title in 1957-58, but was a legitimate contender in 1972-73.

The Razorbacks won three of their first four games and found themselves alone in second with an 8-4 mark when Terry's school-record 47 points burned SMU in a 103-96 win on Feb. 24.

That was Arkansas' fourth straight win and put the team in position to grab a share of the lead with a win over first-place Texas Tech at Barnhill Fieldhouse.

But the Red Raiders clinched the title with a 64-63 nail-bitter over the Razorbacks.

Terry led the conference with a 28.2 scoring average and came up just three points shy of setting an SWC mark for most points scored in a single season.

THE WIZARD AWAITS Although the college basketball world was buzzing about a matchup between UCLA and North Carolina State in 1973-74, the Razorbacks got the first crack at John "The Wizard of Westwood" Wooden and his Bruins dynasty.

For all the points Van Eman's teams put up during his tenure, they never were able to defend as well as he would have liked. That was especially true in the school's worst loss ever, a 117-66 pasting at Ole Miss in his last season.

"We knew UCLA would enhance our schedule and we thought we would be a representative opponent," Van Eman said. "Back then we thought after (Kareem) Abdul Jabbar left, UCLA would come back to being mere mortals. But now they are bigger and better than they were then."

The Razorbacks trotted out seniors Dennis White, Roger Spears and Tolson along with juniors Ricky Medlock and Steve Price in the backcourt to face a team led by Bill Walton.

UCLA, which had won seven straight NCAA titles, rolled up its 76th straight victory by plastering Arkansas, 101-77, after jumping to a 31-12 lead early on.

Walton led UCLA with 23 points and 17 rebounds while Medlock had a game-high 27 points for the Razorbacks.

Van Eman got a car and a win in his last game as coach.

LANNY SAYS GOODBYE Arkansas, 10-16 overall and 6-8 in the SWC in 1973-74, would end up with its third losing season in Van Eman's four years, which caused him to announce late in February with three games still on the slate that he would resign at the end of the season.

Arkansas went on to win two of those three games, including a 97-86 win in Van Eman and Tolson's last game. Tolson set a school record with 20 field goals en route to 45 points on the afternoon.

At halftime, Van Eman was presented with a 1974 Chevrolet and a plaque which read "To a hell of a coach, in tribute to your contribution to U of A basketball."

Eddie Sutton Era

Years Coached: 1974-85; Record 260-75 (.776)

Arkansas Athletic Director Frank Broyles looked to many of the top basketball minds in the country for advice on hiring his next basketball coach, but none were more important than UCLA coach John Wooden.

Wooden suggested Eddie Sutton, the bright and young Creighton coach who had once been a star at Oklahoma State, and Sutton was made the highest paid coach in the Southwest Conference with a five-year contract estimated at $26,000 per year beginning in 1974.

"I feel like the basketball program here is a sleeping giant that is rich in basketball tradition," Sutton said. "It's my job to wake it up."

University of Arkansas Athletic Director Frank Broyles hit the jackpot with the hiring of young Creighton coach Eddie Sutton.

WAKING THE GIANT Sutton took over a program that had posted losing campaigns in nine of the past 11 seasons and had not won a SWC championship since 1958.

The turnaround began immediately with the additions of 6-foot-4 Conway standout Marvin Delph, 6-8 Darryl Saulsberry, 6-7 senior transfer Kent Allison, 6-4 forward

Charles Terry and 6-8 freshman Jim Counce.

That quintet joined a squad that already included returning national free throw champ Ricky Medlock, 6-8 junior forward Jack Schulte, 6-1 junior guard Robert Birden, 6-3 senior guard Steve Price, 6-10 sophomore center Steve Stroud, 6-9 junior center Dan Pauley and 6-4 sophomore guard Syl Allen.

The 1974-75 opener, which featured a preliminary game between Fayetteville and Little Rock Parkview, turned out to be a romp for the Razorbacks.

Saulsberry and Schulte poured in 16 points each and Medlock 13, as Arkansas ripped Rockhurst, 78-61, in a game in which adult tickets were only $2 and $1 for students.

"I'm happy for the win," said Sutton, "but the game went about the way I had anticipated. We executed very well at times, but at times played about as poorly as we could. When our guys see the film some of them are going to be shocked at their performances."

Jack Schulte was a solid performer for Sutton's first team.

A BANNER SWC CAMPAIGN Arkansas finished its preconference season 6-6 before playing host to league favorite Texas Tech in Sutton's first-ever SWC game.

With the spirit group "Mad Hatters" helping lead a crowd of 5,100 fans in what was described as unprecedented crowd enthusiasm, the Razorbacks upset the Red Raiders, 65-62.

Medlock had 16 points, Terry 13 and Allison 12 points and 10 rebounds in the win, which was as big as any they had posted in the last 15 years.

Arkansas led the last 36 minutes of the game, but Terry saved the game when he stole the ball from behind as Tech guard Keith Kitchens went in for a go-ahead layup with 25 seconds left.

The Razorbacks finished 11-3 and in second place by whipping Baylor, 83-64, in the final game of the season.

HONORS, BUT NO INVITE Sutton was named UPI's SWC Coach of the Year and Allison and Birden were tabbed to the all-league team, but the NCAA, NIT and National Commissioners Invitational Tournament in Louisville failed to invite the Razorbacks (17-9).

The 17-9 mark was the best record for an Arkansas team in 27 years.

"I fault the Southwest Conference office more than the selection committee for one of our teams not being invited," Sutton said. "The conference is just not basketball oriented."

ADDING TALENT Sutton continued his overhaul of the program in 1975-76 with the addition of 6-4 guards

Ron Brewer was one of the most gifted offensive performers to ever grace the court for the Razorbacks.

RAZORBACK QUIZ

18. What is the
school record for
consecutive season-
opening wins?

Sidney Moncrief of Little Rock Hall and Ron Brewer of
Westark Community College.

Along with 6-4 sophomore Delph, this gave the
second-year coach a clean sweep of the three best high
school basketball players in the state the last two seasons.

The three combined for 51 points, 27 rebounds and
four blocked shots to highlight Arkansas' 83-57 season-
opening win over Southwest Missouri State.

"It seem like Arkansas has 100 6-4 guys who could
jump almost out of the gym," said SMSU coach Bill
Thomas. "I can see why they're picked in the upper
division of the Southwest Conference. They're an
outstanding basketball team."

Delph averaged 16.3 points to lead the team while
Saulsberry (14.7), Moncrief (12.6) and Brewer (11.9) all
averaged in double figures for the season.

HELLO HOUSTON One of the more memorable games in a
season in which the Razorbacks went 19-9 overall and
finished fourth in the SWC with a 9-7 mark was a
January 1976 bout with new league member Houston.

*Marvin Delph is still
regarded as the best
pure shooter the
school has ever
produced.*

Moncrief had 17 to lead five Arkansas players in double figures in a 92-47 thrashing of the Cougars at Barnhill in a mid-week night game that was broadcast statewide.

The Razorbacks (8-1) handed Houston's the worst loss in school history, a rude awakening for the Cougars in their first SWC game. The only problem was the Razorbacks followed this win with two straight losses, one a 72-71 loss at Houston.

THE END Sutton's second season ended with a 70-63 loss to Texas Tech in the SWC Tournament.

WINNING TWICE

Arkansas' early season play during the 1976-77 season was highlighted by a win on the road at Southwest Missouri State. The game was played before a crowd of 6,618 on hand for the opener

Jim Counce was known for his defense, but had his offensive moments as well.

for the Hammons Student Center, a $5.5 million multi-purpose facility, on the campus of the school located in Springfield, Mo.

"I thought we were going to have another Munich," said Sutton referring to the Olympic gold medal game in 1972 in which the USSR was given three attempts in the final three seconds to beat the USA and finally did.

With six seconds and the Razorbacks leading 70-69, SMSU's Scott Hawk committed his fifth foul. That sent UA's Jim Counce to the line.

Southwest Missouri State coach Bill Thomas substituted quickly even though he had one minute in which to pick a player.

Harry Policape, a 6-7 freshman, was sent into the game, but Thomas was actually sending him in for Charley Moore. The public address announcer, who couldn't hear Policape because of the crowd, just assumed he was going in for Hawk.

He announced the substitution and as Thomas was getting his real sub, Counce missed the free throw and Milton McDonald missed a 55-footer for the Bears as time ran out.

Thomas argued his case for a "correctable error" and the officials eventually came to Arkansas' dressing room some five minutes after the game ended and told the Razorbacks they had to come back out.

"Half of us were already dressed," Counce said.

With the six seconds put back on the clock, Counce stepped up and drilled both free throws. The Arkansas defense then stood motionless as Mark Witherspoon drove for a meaningless free throw.

"In your crooked eye," Counce doubled back to say to the scorer's table.

This was a familiar sight during Sidney Moncrief's high-flying days in Fayetteville.

Rick Bullock led the Red Raiders with a whopping 44 points, including 12 after a controversial foul call. Arkansas led 51-48 with 8:18 left when Saulsberry and Bullock — both with four fouls — collided as Saulsberry went down the lane. The call went against the Razorbacks' center and Bullock took over from that point.

"It was a bad call, but the really horrible call came with ten-and-a-half minutes left when Bullock fouled Darryl and it wasn't called," Sutton said. "Bullock is a great player and had a great night, but he shouldn't have played the last ten-and-a-half minutes of the game."

BOBBY KNIGHT'S WRONG? Indiana head coach Bobby Knight led his unbeaten team to the national title in 1975-76 and also admitted he was wrong.

Knight had told Sutton that he shouldn't take the Arkansas job.

"I was wrong," Knight said. "You made the right

move, you "bleep." I won the national title this year, but so what? Indiana's done it before. But here … here they are going to build statues of you."

1976-77: THE DREAM SEASON

Arkansas would go 26-2, including a 16-0 run through the Southwest Conference.

The only regular-season loss was a 69-62 defeat at the hands of Memphis State in Little Rock in which the Razorbacks committed 29 turnovers.

"We talk about the magic level of intensity and tonight I think both teams went beyond it," Sutton said. "Both wanted to win so emotionally."

Arkansas regrouped in a big way and would not lose again until the NCAA Tournament, but it was not without plenty of close calls.

It took Brewer's 25-foot turnaround jumper at Texas Tech with four seconds left to break open a tie game the Razorbacks eventually won 41-38.

Delph had 24 and Brewer 22 as No. 14 Arkansas pushed its SWC mark to 11-0 and broke Houston's 16-game winning streak at Hofheinz with an 82-80 decision.

THE CLINCHER Arkansas wrapped up the outright SWC title with a 79-64 win at TCU with Brewer pouring in 23, Delph 21, Moncrief 17 and backup center Steve Schall contributing quality minutes.

Some 400 fans were on hand at Drake Field in 20 degree temperatures when the Razorbacks arrived home via plane at 11:45 p.m. to celebrate their first outright league title since 1941.

"This is a great night for us," Sutton said. "And it's a big thrill seeing all these fans here. They share in our success and the team belongs to them. So many people have identified with our basketball success now, after all the years of identifying only with football."

The Razorbacks completed the 16-0 run two games later by edging Texas A&M, 63-62, in a game in which Arkansas set a school record with its 17th straight win and led by as much as 15.

Arkansas held the ball the last 27 seconds as the Aggies failed to either steal the ball or foul.

Brewer, Delph and Moncrief — nicknamed The Three Basketeers at this point but later termed The Triplets by NBC broadcaster Al McGuire — were named All-SWC.

THE NCAA: ONE AND DONE After Brewer's 29 points helped Arkansas whip Houston, 80-74, in the SWC Tournament championship game, the Razorbacks left for a brief stay

RAZORBACK QUIZ

19. Name the largest victory margin by a Razorback squad.

RAZORBACK QUIZ

20. What is the highest total of points an Arkansas team has scored on an opponent's home floor?

The 1977-78 team got Arkansas back to the NCAA Tournament after a 19-year absence.

U.S. Reed was a late summer signee who proved to be a great addition.

at the NCAA Tournament.

They were pitted against Wake Forest in a first-round game at Oklahoma City and raced to a 46-33 halftime lead.

But Moncrief got in foul trouble and became the first of the big three to foul out all season as the Demon Deacons (21-7) rallied for a 86-80 win in game in which Arkansas suffered 23 turnovers.

"I'm not so disappointed from our standpoint," Sutton said. "But the loss bothers me because we were representing our whole league. I know there will be some writers from the East who will just say 'Another Southwest Conference team has gone down to defeat.' "

1977-78: HELLO FINAL FOUR

After big wins against Kansas and LSU in the non-conference portion of the schedule, the Razorbacks got down to business in the SWC.

Riding high with a 14-0 mark and a 32-game regular-season winning streak, No. 4 Arkansas arrived in Austin, Texas, to meet a revved-up group of Longhorns.

The result: A 75-69 Razorback loss in front of a record crowd of 16,288 in the Longhorns' new Super Drum.

"Texas made fewer mistakes and deserved to win," Sutton said. "They played better than we did and we didn't play that badly."

The pair stayed at the top of the SWC standings the entire season and met again in early February in Fayetteville with Texas having a chance to take a two-game lead.

The Longhorns led by as much as 11 in the second half, but Delph's 30 points helped rally the No. 2 Razorbacks to a 75-71 win on a night when Brewer was sick and Moncrief's game was off.

Texas coach Abe Lemons praised both teams for their play, but was upset that he had to wade in mud up to the front door since Arkansas' parking lot was under construction.

"We had to wade up to our bleep in mud to get in here," Lemons said. "Arkansas ought to take some money and pave something. Have people here heard about concrete? I think a foot-wide walkway, or a rope to swing in on would be nice."

The two teams would finish co-champs with 14-2 marks.

Moncrief was a three-time All-SWC player and a two-time All-American.

NO. 1 The Razorbacks were bumped up to No. 1 in the Associated Press poll and Moncrief featured on the cover of *Sports Illustrated* on Feb. 13, 1978.

Arkansas promptly went out and drilled Baylor, 82-56, at Barnhill Arena. Moncrief had 20 points, Brewer 16 and freshman U.S. Reed poured in 13 points to lead the way in the win.

"I feel that being ranked No. 1 in a greater honor for the conference than it is for the school," Sutton said. "I'd like to think every school in the league is proud of us."

Houston wasn't proud enough of the Razorbacks to just let them win in the game that followed five days later. Ken Williams scored 20 points as Houston downed visiting Arkansas, 84-75, before 10,013 fired-up fans.

The two met again in the semifinals of the SWC Tournament, with Cecile Rose's shot with three seconds left giving Houston a 70-69 win. The Cougars then clinched an automatic berth in the NCAA by downing Texas in the final.

Arkansas (28-3) was invited to join Houston in the NCAA Tournament while Texas (22-5) was sent to the NIT, a tournament the Longhorns went on to win.

THE ROAD TO THE CHECKERDOME Arkansas' NCAA appearance this time around lasted quite a bit longer than the one game the Razorbacks played the year before.

It started with a 75-52 rout of Weber State in the NCAA Western Regional in Eugene, Ore. Delph had 20, Moncrief 19 and Brewer 16 in the win.

That set up a tilt in Albuquerque with UCLA, which had edged Kansas, 83-76, in its opener.

RAZORBACK QUIZ

21. What is the fewest number of turnovers in a game by a Razorback team?

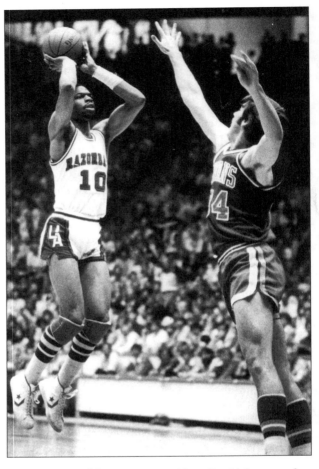

Brewer was as effective inside as he was outside.

Delph's range was from 30 feet in and he was feared by defenses everywhere.

"UCLA would win a series with us," said Sutton, who watched Razorback freshman Michael Whatley leave the team before the game. "Day in and day out they're a better ball club because of depth. But this isn't a series, it's a one-game shot."

Delph had 23, Moncrief 21 and Brewer 18 as the Razorbacks downed the Bruins, 74-70, for the biggest win in school history.

The only concern for Saturday's regional final was Moncrief's availability. He took a hard fall when going in for a slam dunk with 12 seconds left in the UCLA game.

Brewer had 22 points and was named the regional MVP as he led the way in a 61-58 win over Cal-State Fullerton a few days later. His 25-footer with 1:18 left put the Razorbacks ahead 59-58, and then he joined Counce and Moncrief in stopping Keith Anderson's drive to the hoop in the final seconds.

DELPH-LESS Arkansas did not know for a few days if Marvin Delph was going to be able to play in the Final Four at the Checkerdome in St. Louis.

Delph, who had become the leading scorer in Arkansas history, was declared ineligible to play for about 24 hours by Athletic Director Frank Broyles leading up to the event. The punishment stemmed from reports that Conway Chamber of Commerce had raised $1,100 for his parents to fly to Albuquerque to see the game with Cal-State Fullerton.

But the NCAA subcommittee voted to reinstate Delph three days before the game between the Razorbacks (31-3) and No. 1 Kentucky (28-3) because nobody at the school knew what had happened and all the money was returned.

THE FINAL FOUR The Razorback players and their coaches knew how big an event they were part of when they showed up for practice at The Checkerdome.

"We walked into the Checkerdome the day before we played Kentucky and there were 12,000 people there for practice and we played Kentucky before a packed house of 18,000," Sutton said. "I know there are a great many athletic events where you can feel the electricity in the air, but none like the Final Four."

Kentucky spoiled things by beating Arkansas, 64-59, and Duke handled Notre Dame in the other semifinal.

Brewer had 16, Delph 15 and Moncrief 13 for the Razorbacks while Jack Givens led the way for the Wildcats with 23.

Brewer helped Arkansas end the season on a winning note as he hit a turnaround jumper to lift the Razorbacks

22. Who made the pass to Charles Balentine for his shot that beat No. 1 North Carolina and Michael Jordan in Pine Bluff?

Sidney Moncrief and Arkansas governor Bill Clinton were the two most popular men in the state at one time.

Steve Schall and Sidney Moncrief celebrate a SWC Tournament title in 1977.

over Notre Dame, 71-69, in the third-place game.

It was the eighth time in two years that Brewer had scored at the buzzer.

"I like the consolation game a little better now than I did this afternoon," Sutton said. "I had a long talk with the committee and I can understand the value of a third-place game."

1978-79: SUPER SID

James Crockett was given the nickname "Rocket Crockett" in his two years at Arkansas.

With Brewer and Delph off to NBA and Athletes in Action respectively, it left Moncrief to lead the way.

He was joined by 6-foot-11 senior center Schall, junior Alan Zahn, sophomores Reed, Mike Young and James Crockett and a host of talented freshmen including 6-9 forward Scott Hastings.

It would be a season where Moncrief would lead the team to 25-5 mark overall, a share of the SWC title with a 13-3 record and just one win away from a return trip to the Final Four.

Moncrief averaged 22 points and 9.6 seasons in a season in which he was named the SWC Player of the Year and an All-American for the second straight season.

"Sidney's fierce competitive spirit is bound to have a positive effect on our younger players," Sutton said before the season. "He is simply one of the best players in college basketball today."

BATTLING TEXAS AGAIN Arkansas and Texas shared the 1978-79 title once again with 13-3 marks and both teams winning on the other's home court.

The Longhorns snapped the Razorbacks' 35-game winning streak at Barnhill Arena with a 66-63 win as Texas' Jim Krivacs scored 21 points and Johnny Moore 17.

Arkansas returned the favor with a 68-58 win in Austin with Moncrief leading the way with 23 points and Reed adding 15.

The Razorbacks earned a share of the title when Moncrief nailed a 10-footer with six seconds left to lift No. 10 Arkansas over Texas Tech, 66-65, in Lubbock while SMU was upsetting No. 11 Texas, 81-66, in Dallas.

Arkansas shot an unbelievable 79.4 percent from the field, the second best percentage ever in an NCAA game.

SETTLING THE ISSUE Arkansas and Texas then met in their rubber game of season in the SWC Tournament in Houston.

The game came down to a jump ball between Arkansas' 6-foot-7 Zahn and Texas' 6-foot-6 John Danks with the Razorbacks leading 37-36 with 22 seconds left in the game.

Phillip Stroud looked to be coming up with the tip, but U.S. Reed used his speed to get to the ball first and fed Moncrief for a layup and a 39-36 advantage with 16 seconds left. The Longhorns added two points to make the final 39-38.

Moncrief was named the MVP of the tournament.

Best Field Goal Percentage
(8 shot min.)
1.000 Isaiah Morris (8-8) vs Mississippi State 1/15/92
1.000 Daryll Saulsberry (10-10) vs Mac Murray 1/4/75
1.000 Steve Schall (9-9) vs Weber State 3/11/79
1.000 Joe Kleim (8-8) vs St. Peter's 12/28/83

U.S. Reed's jumper finds the range to take down Texas, 60-59.

BARNHILL ARENA

Despite the fact that Arkansas basketball was going through a period in the 1950s when it didn't win any SWC titles, the Razorbacks' popularity continued to increase and brought on the need for a larger home.

First known as Razorback Fieldhouse, the 5,100-seat playing facility seemed just as much for the football team as it did the basketball program. A sawdust workout area for the football team was off to one side and a dirt track surrounded the court.

There were permanent seats on the north side, and bleachers were brought in from the football field for seats on the south side. It was not the best of beginnings as a myriad of mishaps occurred to spoil the new fieldhouse's opening night on Dec. 1, 1955.

The overhead scoreboard came crashing to the floor some two hours before the freshman game, the heat mysteriously went out just minutes into the varsity contest and — most disappointingly — the Southeast Oklahoma Savages nipped the Razorbacks, 65-64.

Then UA sports information director Bob Cheyne described the scene years later to a reporter before the last game in Barnhill on March 3, 1993.

"I came by that afternoon around 3 and the scoreboard had fallen," said Cheyne, who joined Wally Ingalls to call the action for radio. "It scarred the middle of the floor. For two games we kept score by writing with chalk on a green chalkboard. Today, you couldn't do that because teams score too fast."

Razorback Fieldhouse was renamed Barnhill Fieldhouse in 1957 after the man who is given credit for being the architect of the Razorback program. That's John Barnhill, who came to Arkansas from Tennessee in 1946 and was head football coach for four years. He took a pay cut in 1949 to become the full-time athletic director.

Barnhill rallied the people of Arkansas around the Razorbacks by building a statewide radio network, drawing support from all over the corners of the state and involving people all over the state in the program.

By the time Eddie Sutton was hired to coach the Razorbacks in 1974, the program had slid to a point to where it was something of an afterthought for many fans.

"When I got there (Arkansas),

THE WORD ABOUT BARNHILL ARENA

"You don't have memories of the place," former TCU head coach Jim Killingsworth said. *"Just the nightmares."*

"Undoubtedly the toughest place in the country to play," noted Pat Foster, who returned when he was head coach of the University of Houston.

"I can't think of a tougher place to take a team than Barnhill," said former Texas A&M head coach Shelby Metcalf. *"Absolutely the worst thing that could happen was to get beat, get snowed in and not be able to get out of town."*

"I don't think I've ever seen officials get intimidated as badly as they did in Barnhill," legendary Texas coach Abe Lemons surmised. *"They didn't mean to. It just happened."*

---

you could shoot a gun in the arena at 7 o'clock prior to tip-off, and you wouldn't hit anybody," Sutton said. "We didn't even have a pep band there. I had to pay them $5 each to show up and play."

Sutton, coming off an NCAA Tournament appearance at Creighton, got Broyles to promise he would either renovate or replace Barnhill Fieldhouse before he would accept the job.

After 17-9 and 19-9 seasons, Sutton got the first phase of an $8 million renovation. The first stage, completed in 1977, raised the seating capacity from 5,000 to 6,200 and the building had permanent seating on the south side for the first time.

The second phase, completed after a 26-2 season in 1976-77 that saw the Razorbacks earn their first NCAA berth in 19 years, took the seating capacity up to 9,000.

During this time Sutton hired Jim Robken to direct the Hog Wild band and an intimidating

atmosphere was born.

Tulsa World columnist Bill Connors wrote that it was like "Rosanne Barr turning into Cindy Crawford overnight."

Arkansas would go on to win 313 of its 416 games played in Barnhill, which was named as one of the 10 toughest places to play in a article by *Inside Sports*.

The longest winning streak in the building was 24 games. The Razorbacks lost just an average of 2.7 games per year in the building's 38 seasons — something that is even more astounding when you realize the 1970-71 team lost 11 games in Barnhill.

They were undefeated in six of those seasons and they also lost just six of their last 83 games in Barnhill and were 188-22 after the renovations.

It was certainly impressive to the coaches who brought their teams inside what became known as the toughest place to play in the Southwest Conference.

Arkansas beat LSU, 88-75, in the last game played at Barnhill Arena in March 3, 1993.

MONCRIEF VS. BIRD Arkansas bounced Weber State (74-63) in Lawrence, Kan., and Louisville (73-62) in Cincinnati in its first two NCAA Midwest Regional games to set up a regional final matchup with unbeaten Indiana State.

The Sycamores (31-0) were led by 6-9 multi-talented forward Larry Bird, considered the best basketball player in the nation.

Bird had 31 points and 10 rebounds and Moncrief 24 points and eight rebounds as the two dueled in a magnificent game that came down to the final seconds.

Moncrief didn't start defensively on Bird, but held him to two field goals in the final 12:50 after taking over for Zahn.

"Bird is the toughest big man I have ever guarded," said Moncrief. "But it's hard to score if you don't have the ball. I had to keep him from getting it."

With the score tied 71-71 with 1:04 left in the game and Arkansas holding for a final shot, Reed was called for traveling when he was tripped by ISU's Carl Nicks.

"Nicks fouled Reed," Sutton said. "We had them on the ropes. But they didn't call the foul and that's part of the game."

That gave Indiana State a chance to win, but when Bird was bottled up by Moncrief, the Sycamores had to go to Bob Heaton. His left-handed scoop shot in the lane with two seconds left gave ISU a 73-71 victory.

"I really wanted a national championship and we had the material to do it," Moncrief said. "It was like the whole world crashing down on me."

POST TRIPLETS Arkansas went into the 1979-80 season without any of The Triplets who had led them to so much success in the past four years, but Sutton's program survived.

Reed, Hastings and Zahn were three upperclassman who led the way to a 21-8 season, a campaign that included a 13-3 second-place finish in the SWC.

WORKING OVERTIME During the SWC season, Arkansas played the longest game in school history on a February 1980 trip into Houston.

Houston won 90-84 in three overtimes as Larry Rogers scored 28 points to lead Coach Guy V. Lewis' team to the victory over the Razorbacks (17-5, 10-2).

"You talk about gutting it up and playing 40 minutes — well we gutted it up and played for 55," Lewis said. "It was a great game for the spectators and the television audience. Our club showed a lot of character. I've felt all along we could play with anyone in the league."

RAZORBACK QUIZ

23. How many conference championships has Arkansas won?

RAZORBACK QUIZ

24. In what year was Barnhill Fieldhouse constructed?

REED'S HEROICS Arkansas grabbed a first-place tie with Texas A&M a game later by edging the Aggies, 45-44, before a packed house at Barnhill Arena.

With four seconds left and the Razorbacks trailing 44-43, Reed was fouled by A&M center Rudy Woods. He missed the first free throw, but hit the second to deadlock things.

The game appeared headed for overtime, but Dave Goff was whistled for charging when he heaved a desperation shot and bowled over Reed.

Reed stepped to the line and buried the free throw with no time left to give Arkansas the win and tie them at 11-2 atop the SWC with the Aggies.

"Reed made a great play and it was a gutty call by the official," Sutton said. "There's no doubt it was a foul and the film will prove it."

It was the Razorbacks' third last-second win in five games, including Mike Young's 15-foot game-winner at Texas Tech and a buzzer-beater by Reed that downed Texas, 60-59, 10 days earlier on the same court.

Eugenen Nash is still the most popular non-scholarship player in school history.

Scott Hastings lifts U.S. Reed after Reed's free throw with no time left beat Texas A&M, 45-44.

"It looks like we are the masters of winning at the buzzer," Zahn said.

Arkansas finished a game behind A&M in the SWC race and then lost to the Aggies, 52-50, in the SWC Tournament.

Kansas State then eliminated Arkansas, 71-53, in an NCAA Tournament first-round game. It was the worst loss in six years for a Sutton team.

RAZORBACK QUIZ

25. Name the most popular player to ever walk-on at Arkansas.

THE GREAT ALASKAN SHOOTOUT No Arkansas team has gotten off to a better start against quality competition in a season-opener than the 1980-81 team against Missouri.

With sophomore transfer Darrell Walker and Reed causing havoc in the backcourt, the Razorbacks raced to a 40-9 lead over the Tigers before holding on for a 81-73 lead.

Arkansas then whipped LSU, 86-76, before falling to North Carolina, 64-58, in the championship game.

All the games were broadcast live back to Arkansas and the late night ratings were tremendous.

"We had the toughest road to hoe in this tournament and you can't measure the toil that takes on a team," Arkansas assistant coach Jim Counce said. "But we realize we can play with the best teams in the country now."

AN SWC TURNAROUND At one point in the 1980-81 season, Arkansas found itself 2-3 in SWC action and losers of three in a row to Texas, Baylor and Houston. But the Razorbacks won their last 11 games to finish with a 13-3 mark and the outright league title.

Arkansas took over the lead for good with a 65-61 victory over Texas A&M in College Station on Feb. 17 in a game that sometimes resembled a heavyweight fight.

Reggie Roberts and Darrell Walker squared off; Aggie Claude Riley was ejected for taking a swing at Hastings, and teammate Roy Jones was assessed a two-shot foul for elbowing Hastings with seven seconds left.

Arkansas' 11-game win streak came to the end when Texas upset the No. 14 Razorbacks, 76-73, in the semifinals of the SWC Conference Tournament in San Antonio.

RAZORBACK QUIZ

26. How many times did the Razorbacks go to the Final Four before the 1990s?

THE SHOT You could not get very many Razorback fans to tell you exactly what happened during the 1981 NCAA Tournament except for one shot.

That would be Reed's 49-foot heave from halfcourt against Louisville that found nothing but net and a place in Arkansas basketball lore.

The Razorbacks, who had downed Mercer, 73-67, in the first round of the NCAA Tournament in Austin, fell

Hastings' shot over Akeem Olajuwon set off bedlam in Barnhill Arena.

behind 73-72 when Derek Smith hit a nine-foot putback with just five seconds left.

Reed got the ball inbounds and began to dribble upcourt with the defense coming to halfcourt to meet him. He looked at the clock, saw :02 and let fly from 49 feet away.

Reed, ever the cool one, just walked over to the scorer's table and shook hands with Ish Haley, a former Arkansas sportswriter who was now working in Dallas.

"I was just so happy I started shaking hands," Reed said. "Like a new father or something. Last year I got hurt when people piled on me after the Texas game, so I wanted to be careful."

LSU then ended the Razorback season with a 72-56 win before an NCAA Tournament-record crowd of 34,036 in New Orleans. Most of the fans were LSU backers.

"The crowd didn't affect our team," Reed said, "but it sure got LSU going."

Entering the 1996-97 season, LSU has yet to beat Arkansas in 10 tries since the Razorbacks joined the SEC.

HASTINGS HAUNTS HOUSTON

Arkansas trailed No. 19 Houston by 10 points with less than seven minutes left to go in a key SWC regionally televised game in Barnhill Arena on Jan. 23, 1982.

Darrell Walker made an impact on the defensive end from his first game as a Razorback.

But the No. 15 Razorbacks rallied to tie the game 62-62 and had a chance to win when Keith Peterson stole the ball from Clyde Drexler with 31 seconds left.

Hastings then canned a 22-footer over the outstretched arm of 7-foot-1 Akeem Olajuwon with five seconds left to give Arkansas the win.

"I never watched the ball when I shot, but I watched this one," Hastings said. "I knew it had good rotation. I think it was a swish. It was kinda fun."

WALKER DOES IN A&M Darrell Walker had never been known as a great shooter, but he was always known as a player who would do whatever it took to win.

That's why no one was surprised when Walker canned a 21-foot jumper with two seconds left to beat Texas A&M, 64-63, in College Station just four days after the win over Houston.

"Darrell has been the subject of a lot of praise and lot of criticism," Counce said. "But he played his heart out tonight and made a championship play. He's literally exhausted right now. At the end, he took it on himself to say 'I'm gonna win it or lose it myself.'"

Abe Lemons looks for a piece of Walker after an altercation that occurred in the Arkansas-Texas game.

THE LIGHTNING ROD It seemed that Walker was always involved in controversy, but never more than after a hard-fought 62-55 overtime win over Texas at Barnhill on Feb. 6, 1982.

Darrell Walker's intensity was one of the things that made him a lightning rod for opponent's attentions.

Hastings had 22 points and Walker 15 in a game in which tempers flared when Hastings went in for a dunk with 18 seconds remaining.

Hastings was hammered by A&M's Virdell Howland and the two squared off. Walker then popped Texas guard Ray Harper with a punch and was kicked out of the game.

It was later revealed on film from a Springfield, Mo., television station that Harper had raced around Walker and pushed Hastings before Walker unloaded on him.

"He (Harper) was out there trying to take cheap shots, really sneaky," Walker said. "I'm not going to lose any sleep over it."

Texas coach Abe Lemons was outraged and rushed the court and yelled at Walker. He later got into it with Arkansas fans behind the bench and was on his way to the locker room when a near brawl broke out. He threw a punch that actually missed a Razorback fan and hit one of his team's officials in the stomach.

RAZORBACK QUIZ

27. What pro teams did Nolan Richardson try out for after his college career?

"If the league doesn't suspend him (Walker), they've got no guts," Lemons said.

The SWC conducted an investigation and Arkansas gathered film to support its claim that it was Harper who instigated the action. Walker was reprimanded, but missed no action.

Walker later raced to the bench and sat down on the floor when a potential melee broke out later in a 92-75 win over Texas A&M that gave the Razorbacks a game lead over the Aggies late in the season.

"Next time I'll bring a magazine," Walker said. "It was like I was at a movie; I wished I had some popcorn."

TWO MORE TITLES In a game in which Sutton started wildly popular senior walk-on Eugene Nash and fellow senior Greg Skulman, the Razorbacks wrapped up the 1981-82 SWC title with a win over Texas Tech.

Hastings had 17 points and Walker 14 points and seven steals to lead the way as Arkansas (12-4) downed the Red Raiders, 67-61, and outdistanced Houston by a game.

The Razorbacks, with 9,000 of their closest friends on hand at "Barnhill South" in Dallas, then took the SWC Tournament title with an 84-69 win over Houston.

Alvin Robertson, Arkansas' sixth man during the season, was named the MVP of the tournament after scoring 37 points in the two games while drawing only his third and fourth starts of the season.

He had 23 points in the final, but felt Hastings deserved to be MVP.

"I'm so proud for our seniors," Sutton said. "This really means a lot because of them."

K-STATE AGAIN Kansas State continued its hex over the Razorbacks by edging them, 65-64, in the first round of the NCAA Tournament in Dallas.

Hastings missed a 20-footer with three seconds left and the Wildcats had their fourth straight win over the Razorbacks (23-6, 12-4).

REBUILDING AND HOW Although Darrell Walker and Alvin Robertson were the only players with much experience returning for Sutton in 1982-83, Arkansas had one of its better seasons.

That was because of a talented influx of players that included sophomore transfer centers Joe Kleine of Notre Dame and 7-1 Shaheed Ali, seniors John Snively and Carey Kelly, juniors Leroy Sutton, Ricky Norton, Robert Kitchen and Robert Brannen, sophomore Charles Balentine and freshmen Willie Cutts, Kennan Debose, Darryl Bedford and Eric Poerschke.

RAZORBACK QUIZ

28. Arkansas trainer Dave England worked with what major league baseball organization before joining the Razorbacks?

RAZORBACK QUIZ

29. What is the lowest scoring game in UA history?

Alvin Robertson continued the long line of Arkansas guards under Sutton who were defensive stars.

This group ripped off a 25-2 regular season with the only two losses coming at the hands of SWC champion and No. 1-ranked Houston, which would go on to play in the NCAA championship game.

SWC CHAMPIONSHIP Arkansas and Houston entered the next-to-last conference clash with the Razorbacks still clinging to hopes of a share of the SWC title.

But the No. 1 Cougars won their 19th straight with Olajuwon leading the way with 15 points and nine rebounds in the 74-66 victory at Barnhill Arena.

Kleine had 20 points and 10 rebounds to lead Arkansas.

"We didn't feel like we were No. 1 until we beat Arkansas in Fayetteville," said Houston volunteer coach Terry Kirkpatrick, whose team had lost seven straight at

Arkansas' gain was Notre Dame's loss when Joe Kleine brought his talent from South Bend to Fayetteville.

Barnhill. "There's a certain mystique they had and have here. The UA is a great organization — a class machine — and Eddie Sutton is a class coach."

THE POSTSEASON A third meeting in the 1982-83 season between the Razorbacks and the Cougars never materialized because TCU edged Arkansas, 61-59 in overtime, before 17,057 fans in an SWC Tournament semifinal.

The Razorbacks led 51-40 with 5:40 left, but lost when Darrell Browder cashed in two free throws with four seconds left to seal the upset.

Arkansas won its last nine SWC Tournament games.

"I just wish TCU had beaten us all the way down the line, rather than us just messing up the game," Sutton said.

Arkansas then beat Purdue, 78-68, in the first round of the NCAA Tournament in Tampa as Robertson scored 26 points and eight steals.

The season ended a game later when No. 2 Louisville's Scooter McCray tipped in a shot with one second left to edge Arkansas, 65-63.

"I guess turnabout is fair play," Louisville head coach

Denny Crum said. "Ours was a six-incher and theirs (in 1981) was a 50-footer, but they both counted two points."

TAKING ON THE CHAMP

Arkansas started the 1983-84 season in Alaska once again and quickly dismissed Fordham (62-61) and Oklahoma (84-78) to set up a championship game matchup with defending national champion North Carolina State.

The Wolfpack claimed the crown with a 65-60 win despite 18 points from MVP Joe Kleine and solid performance from Balentine (14 points) and Robertson (13).

"The only negative," Arkansas assistant Bill Brown said, "is that feel we are a better basketball team (than N.C. State). That makes it tough. We're also thinking about the long ride home."

Bill Brown was one of Eddie Sutton's trusted aides and a very popular coach.

BALENTINE'S DAY

After whipping SMU (80-71) in Dallas on Saturday, the Razorbacks hopped a plane and flew to Pine Bluff for a Feb. 12 clash with No. 1 North Carolina a day later.

Several of the Razorbacks became ill on the plane. This was not good news since they would have to play a Tar Heel lineup that featured Michael Jordan and Sam Perkins.

The fans at the Pine Bluff Convention Center got their money's worth with Jordan, who had 21 points, scoring six straight points to put his team up 64-63 with 1:13 left. It was the first North Carolina lead in 23 minutes.

With time running down, Robertson hit Balentine on the baseline with a pass and the Newport native canned an eight-footer over Perkins.

Balentine's shot put Arkansas up 65-64 and North Carolina's Steve Hale put up a 22-footer that bounced off

Charles Balentine gets a hero's welcome at the Fayetteville airport after his shot helped Arkansas upset No. 1 North Carolina on Feb. 12, 1984.

Darryl Bedford's first moment as a Razorback was in the upset of No. 1 North Carolina.

Sutton's last year at Arkansas was filled with turmoil.

the rim at the buzzer to hand the Razorbacks the upset.

"I got the ball and Perkins jumped in my way to cut off the baseline," Balentine said. "I just prayed the ball would go in."

Kleine had 20 points, freshman Darryl Bedford 12 off the bench, Leroy Sutton 11 points, Robertson 10 assists and Balentine 10.

"This one (win) certainly ranks near the top," Sutton said. "No Arkansas team had ever beaten a No. 1 team. I'm very proud of our players."

THE DREAM VS. THE NIGHTMARE NBC hyped a late-season matchup between Houston and visiting Arkansas as Akeem "The Dream" Olajuwon vs. Joe "The Nightmare" Kleine.

Olajuwon had 19 points and 10 rebounds and Kleine 17 points and 11 rebounds in a pairing of two of the nation's top centers.

Houston (14-0 in SWC action) won the game, 64-61, to take a two-game lead over Arkansas with two games

to play.

Arkansas couldn't make up that difference, but did cap its regular season by beating the Cougars, 73-68, at Barnhill.

Kleine had 22 points while holding Olajuwon to just 10, but it was Balentine's 16 points that made the difference.

The rubber match between the two teams occurred in the SWC Tournament and Olajuwon got his revenge with 20 points, 11 rebounds and 10 blocks as Houston edged Arkansas, 57-56.

"I just hope we can meet for a fourth time," Sutton said.

That did not happen because Virginia's Rick Carlise buried a 12-foot baseline jumper with four seconds left in overtime to oust Arkansas, 53-51.

The Razorbacks finished the season with a 25-7 record.

RAZORBACK QUIZ

30. What was the longest losing streak Arkansas has ever suffered through?

GOLDEN BOYS Both Kleine and Robertson were selected to play on the USA Olympic basketball team at the 1984 Summer Olympics in Los Angeles, which were boycotted by the USSR.

The team, which also featured Jordan and Georgetown's Patrick Ewing, routed Spain in the gold medal game, 96-65, with Jordan pumping in 20 points.

"It's not a big disappointment the Russians are not here," Jordan said. " We would have won the gold medal anyway. I think we could beat the Russians anywhere, anytime."

A SEASON OF TURMOIL The 1984-85 season would prove to be Eddie Sutton's last at Arkansas, and it was a campaign filled with turmoil and an unprecedented 13 losses — the most in his 11-year tenure.

It was a 22-13 season (10-6 in SWC action) where he had to fend off reports that he was headed elsewhere and that he was feuding with Athletic Director Frank Broyles.

It would end with him "crawling to Kentucky" after losing in the SWC Tournament finals to Texas Tech despite Kleine's 36 points and whipping Iowa and falling to St. John's in the NCAA Tournament.

Sutton's last game in Barnhill was a 106-71 rout of Baylor. He would return only to clean out his desk after taking the vacant Kentucky post. Sutton said he "would have crawled all the way to Lexington" just two weeks after telling the Arkansas legislature he wanted to retire in Arkansas.

"All my life I have grown to be a point where this is where I belong," Sutton said at a press conference in Kentucky. "This is where I want to be."

RAZORBACK QUIZ

31. Who is the school's all-time leading scorer?

Rollin' With Nolan

Years Coached: 1985-present; Record 272-95 (.746)

Nolan Richardson

Tulsa coach Nolan Richardson took over at Arkansas after Eddie Sutton left for Kentucky.

The last time the Arkansas basketball head coaching job came open, Razorback Athletic Director Frank Broyles really didn't have a surplus of great candidates.

Times had changed when Eddie Sutton bolted to Kentucky in 1985 and Broyles embarked on a new search.

"Eleven years ago, I don't think I had two (bonafide) applications," Broyles said. "I think it is over 25 now from the East Coast to the West Coast and from South to North."

The names mentioned at the time included some of the brightest young coaches including Duke's Mike Krzyzewski, Georgia Tech's Bobby Cremins, Tulsa's Nolan Richardson and Boston College's Gary Williams.

Others whose names popped up in connection with the job included Lamar's Pat Foster, Purdue's Gene Keady, Louisiana Tech's Andy Russo, Illinois State's Bob Donewald, South Florida's Lee Rose, Wyoming's Jim Brandenburg and Virginia Commonwealth's J.D. Barnett, who showed up to interview unannounced.

Richardson, who had a junior college national championship and an NIT title on his resume, became a favorite early on after his interview, according to one insider.

"He had a tremendous interview," said the UA source. "He was articulate, had a quick wit, knew the answers before the questions and had Frank on the edge of his seat while he was talking. Unless someone really dynamic comes along, I don't see how you could go wrong with Nolan."

Broyles apparently saw it the same way and, after a brief flirtation with Villanova head coach Rollie Massimino, offered Richardson the job.

Richardson, whose daughter Yvonne was diagnosed with leukemia a month before the 1984-85 season ended, hesitated because of his daughter's health.

"I wasn't going to take the job because of her," Richardson said. "I thought we have the facilities here in Tulsa to take care of her and I can't take her away from that. But she begged me to take the job and talked about what we could get accomplished with an on-campus facility and what Arkansas offered a coach."

Richardson, whose up-tempo style produced a 119-37 record at Tulsa, thus replaced Sutton and began

Richardson's polka-dotted towel has been a staple on the sidelines since he arrived at Arkansas.

immediately talking of taking Arkansas to the top.

Nolan Richardson is the only coach in history to have won a junior college national title, an NIT title, and an NCAA championship.

"I inherit a tremendous program that always ranks in the Top 20 in the United States," Richardson said. "The challenge at Tulsa was building a program. Now it is reaching for the top.

"I'm not talking about winning Southwest Conference championships. My goal is to win it all. I've won the national championship in junior college. I've won the NIT. I need the big grandfather.

"I'm not a politician and I'm not here to make promises. But I do feel like I must make one here, however. We will be there."

THE POLKA DOTS Richardson wore polka-dotted ties and carried a polka-dotted towel in Tulsa and was the king of self-promotion as he picked Golden Hurricane basketball up off the mat.

The polka dots were quickly adopted by his new state as the fans became excited about the possibility of an up-tempo team.

Scott Rose was Nolan Richardson's first point guard at Arkansas.

THE OVERHAUL BEGINS Perhaps the biggest victory Richardson had in his first season, 1985-86, was off the court and not on it.

He signed Memphis standout Ron Huery, a 6-foot-6 guard from Memphis who had been dubbed Sir Jam-A-Lot when he won a high school dunk contest while he was in the eighth grade.

He would also add 6-10 Oklahoma State transfer Shawn Baker, 6-9 forward Mario Credit, 6-2 sharpshooter Cannon Whitby, 6-7 forward Larry Marks, 6-5 Phillip McKellar and junior college standouts Tim Scott and Anthony Hurd before recruiting was done.

"That was as big as anything we did that year," Richardson said. "That first team will always be my favorite because of the way they fought even if they weren't very good. But adding this class, especially Ron, at least let us know there would be a talent influx coming soon."

Ron Huery was a prized signee and opened the door for Richardson in Memphis.

A FAST START Preseason SWC favorite Arkansas ripped out to a 5-0 start under Richardson although the wins came over schools that were less than powerhouses in Southern Illinois, San Diego State, Southwest Missouri State, Southern and Samford.

"Look at the teams we were beating," Richardson said in 1996. "They were not that good and we were sneaking out with one-point wins over teams like Southern and Southwest Missouri State. We weren't very talented and were just barely getting by."

AN SWC COLLAPSE The SWC-opener with SMU in Fayetteville rammed that point home. Just days after being pummeled by Oklahoma, 92-69, the Mustangs rode into Barnhill and came out with a 71-66 win.

Road losses to TCU and Texas and home losses to Texas Tech (48-46) and Houston (87-85) left the preseason favorite 0-5 and the fans and Richardson thoroughly frustrated.

"The Fat Lady hasn't sung yet, but she is warming up," said Richardson, who also saw 6-11 center Andrew Lang break his hand during this skid.

Arkansas, 121-8 at Barnhill in Sutton's era, would lose four more at home that season and ended the campaign with a 4-12 league mark.

32. How many times have the Razorbacks topped the 100-point mark in a game?

OFF AND RUNNING Unlike 1985-86, when Arkansas barely slipped by its opponents while getting off to a fast start, the 1986-87 Razorbacks came out of the chute strong.

The Razorbacks ripped through Grambling (84-65), Louisiana Tech (90-64) and Ole Miss (70-56) to set up a showdown with No. 6 Kansas and All-American Danny Manning in Fayetteville.

Manning lived up to his billing with a 26-point, 17-rebound effort, but newcomer Scott was the one who took center stage in a game that was broadcast to the nation by ESPN.

Scott buried four three-pointers and 12 of his 13 free throws en route to a 34-point outing that helped Arkansas erase a two-point halftime deficit and roll to a 103-86 win.

The Jayhawks were the highest ranked team to fall in Barnhill Arena in five decades.

"That was just a great win and showed our fans that the program would be back sooner than later," Richardson said. "But we played better that night than we really were, so maybe it did put expectations a little too high."

Arkansas would end its non-conference showing at 9-3, including wins over Ohio State and California in the Rainbow Classic in Hawaii.

A BAD HABIT For the second straight season, Arkansas couldn't open the SWC race with success as TCU whipped the Razorbacks in Fort Worth, 80-77.

At least Arkansas didn't fall into the 0-5 hole that it did the previous season.

Arkansas — which finished 8-8 in the SWC and had another one-game exit in the SWC Classic — would make it into the postseason with an 18-12 mark, courtesy of a 9-2 mark at home.

ASU VS. ARKANSAS During the middle of the 1986-87 season, the state legislature began working on a bill that would force Arkansas State, Arkansas, UALR and the defending Arkansas Intercollegiate champion to play in a midseason tournament.

Arkansas State officials wanted this to happen badly while Arkansas and UALR officials wanted nothing to do with it and wanted any meeting between the teams to happen in postseason action, a long-standing policy of the UA.

Despite support from Governor Bill Clinton, the legislature sent the bill back to committee, where it has not seen the light of day since.

But it just so happens that Arkansas and Arkansas State were matched up in the first round of the NIT Tournament in 1987.

The state senate quickly approved a resolution reading, "Friday night will find the eyes of all Arkansans riveted to their television sets, adrenaline flowing, children neglected and the fate of the world temporarily out of mind."

There were some media outlets in Arkansas that speculated that if the Razorbacks lost, it would be the last game for Richardson.

That prompted Athletic Director Frank Broyles, President Ray Thornton and Chancellor Dan Ferritor to

RAZORBACK QUIZ

33. What player has the all-time highest Razorback single-season rebound average?

RAZORBACK QUIZ

34. In what game did Arkansas attempt a school-record 101 field goals?

pop in at Richardson's house four hours before the game.

"The three of them came over and I had no idea what they were going to say," Richardson said. "I thought maybe they were coming to tell me this was it. I was thinking I still had four years left on my contract and they would have to pay me and I could get a job somewhere else."

But that was not what the trio had in mind at all.

"Thornton said I know you have been reading and hearing things on the radio, but I don't care what they have been writing or saying, you are going to be our basketball coach win, lose or draw," Richardson said. "He said I want you to know that and (wife) Rose to know that."

THE GAME ITSELF Arkansas State, which received 1,700 tickets for the game in Fayetteville, jumped out to a 29-20 lead at half and looked primed for a major upset

Chancellor Dan Ferritor has always been a big supporter of Nolan Richardson's.

Mario Credit was a inside scoring force for Richardson's teams.

Stephan Moore was an explosive jumper and physical force.

when it grabbed a 51-30 lead with 10:43 left in the game.

With the score at 54-37 with 6:37 left, Richardson inserted Cannon Whitby and Arkansas, playing without injured center Andrew Lang, came to life. Huery scored and Whitby ripped off two three-pointers — the second from 30 feet out — to suddenly cut the deficit to 54-45.

Two free throws by Reggie Gordon with 4:02 left put ASU back up by 11, 58-47, at the 4:02 mark, but Huery's three-pointer, two free throws by Whitby and a steal and layup by Mike Ratliff cut it to 58-54.

ASU would hit only one of six free throws in the final 2:09, and Huery first bombed in a three-pointer and then

Cannon Whitby's long three-pointers were key in the comeback win over ASU.

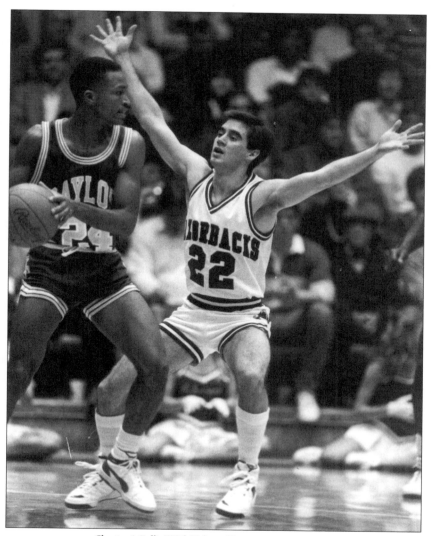

tied the game 59-59 on a 19-footer with 59 seconds left that would send the game into overtime.

Steve Wiedower's three-pointer gave the Indians a 64-63 lead with 2:01 left in overtime, but Mario Credit answered on the other end and a Huery steal and Stephen Moore slam with 34 seconds left sealed the deal.

Arkansas State could not get a shot off in its final two possessions.

"My freshman team won it," Richardson said. "It was all the kids that weren't from Arkansas and really didn't feel the pressure of how big a game it was. That was a big turnaround for the program and we were off and running from that point on."

Homestanding Nebraska ended the Razorbacks' season at 19-14 with a five-point win in the second round of the NIT.

Yvonne Richardson was beloved by her father's team.

THE BIGGEST LOSS Although his basketball team righted its ship on the court, Richardson suffered the biggest loss of his life off the court as his daughter Yvonne died after waging a valiant fight with leukemia.

She died in a Tulsa hospital on Jan. 22 and was laid to rest three days later.

"She will always be a great inspiration to me and to those she came in contact with," Richardson said. "She was a brave little girl who fought to the very end."

1987-88: THE FAVORITE, AGAIN

For the third straight season, Arkansas was tabbed as the preseason favorite despite the fact that it had finished seventh and fifth in the previous two seasons.

"Here's a team that nobody in the league can touch talent-wise, anyway," Houston coach Pat Foster said. "If there has ever been a clear-cut favorite in the league, it's Arkansas.

"They're as much above the league as Houston was when it had the good teams in the early 1980s. They are not as good as Houston, but they are capable of being."

The Razorbacks lived up to their billing in the non-conference portion of the schedule by ripping off nine wins in 11 games, with victories against Virginia and Alabama and losses to Tulsa and Maryland.

Larry Marks was a strong rebounder.

OFF AND RUNNING, AGAIN Arkansas ended its first-game SWC hex by blasting Texas, 91-62, before a raucous Barnhill crowd as Larry Marks poured in 19 points and Tim Scott 18.

The Razorbacks soon moved their record to 3-0 with a 85-83 win in overtime at SMU, which led Arkansas by 22 points with 15:40 left in the game. Huery pumped in

28 points in the win.

Arkansas would continue to have its share of success in the SWC season and ended the campaign in second at 11-5, including going 3-3 down the stretch.

OFF THE SNIDE Arkansas fans continued to come out in record numbers to the SWC Classic at Reunion Arena in Dallas, and the Razorbacks finally gave them a reward for their wait. Matched in a first-round game with Texas A&M, Arkansas ripped through the Aggies, 76-64, before a throng of Razorback fans. Keith Wilson pumped in 18 points and Andrew Lang 14 for the Razorbacks.

"Now the ghost is gone," Richardson said.

Ron Huery was an All-SWC pick in 1988.

Baylor edged Arkansas, 74-73, in the semifinals. The final basket was the Bears' first lead of the game.

THE NCAA RETURNS The win over Texas A&M apparently was good enough to get 11th-seeded Arkansas (21-8) into the NCAA tournament, where it was pitted against 1985 national champion and sixth-seeded Villanova (21-12) in the NCAA Southeast Regional at Cincinnati.

"It's great for Arkansas' program to be back in the NCAA," Richardson said. "Our coaching staff has worked extremely hard to get our team back in this position. The invitation is a tribute to our team, which I feel should play well in the NCAA."

All-SWC pick Huery had 19 of his 21 in the first half and the Razorbacks forced 20 turnovers during their contest, which saw the Wildcats take a 11-point second half lead.

The Razorbacks cut that to one, but Villanova ended up winning, 82-74.

OHIO STATE INQUIRES Ohio State made a big push to hire Richardson after the 1987-88 season, and he was tempted to take the big contract offer because of the problems he had experienced since taking over at Arkansas.

In the end, it was an outpouring of love and affection from the Razorback fans at a local celebrity golf tournament and his desire to finish a job he had started that kept him in Fayetteville.

"I considered Ohio State a lot and there was a time I thought I was going to leave," Richardson said. "But I had brought some kids I had a commitment to, I had not finished what I thought I could do and the fans really made me feel wanted. At that point, it really didn't matter what they offered me."

PROVING A POINT Nolan Richardson has always been a driven man, but a comment — or actually a no comment — burned in his gut all summer long.

As Arkansas made its second one-game exit at the SWC Classic, UA Athletic Director Frank Broyles was asked by reporters about Richardson's status.

"No comment," was all Broyles said.

This didn't sit well with Richardson and he renewed his intention to not only own the SWC Classic, but the regular season as well.

"That bothered me," Richardson said. "He had every right to say it that way, but I'm just a little bit different than most people. If I'm on your team, I'm on your team. If I'm not, I'm not. There is no in between."

That spurred Richardson to make a promise to his team.

RAZORBACK QUIZ

35. What Razorback hit a 58-footer as time ran out in the first half of the Final Four in 1995?

RAZORBACK QUIZ

36. Name the Syracuse player who prolonged Arkansas' 1994-95 NCAA Tournament run.

"I said at that point we are going to own this," Richardson. "Every time you walk in here from now on, there will be no doubt who is going to win this thing. Absolutely no doubt. There is a lot to be said for attitude."

The Razorbacks would never lose another SWC Classic game while racing to three straight championships.

1988-89: TAKING OVER

Despite an off-season that would see junior-to-be Ron Huery make headlines for legal problems and ultimately miss the season to redshirt and assistant Andy Stoglin leave to pursue other options, the Razorbacks took firm grasp of the SWC for their final four years in the league.

This taking over coincided with the arrival of the second set of Arkansas Triplets — the freshman trio of guard Lee Mayberry, forward Todd Day and center Oliver Miller.

Keith Wilson was one of the all-time quickest Razorbacks.

Mike Anderson was a player for Richardson at Tulsa and has been on his staff from the start at Arkansas.

That trio headed up a 25-7 squad in which 10 of the 16 players on the roster had never played one minute of major college basketball. There were six true freshmen, two redshirt freshmen and two junior college transfers, including tremendously talented Lenize Howell, a 6-4 small forward.

"These are all my kids now," said Richardson, who elevated Mike Anderson to a full-time assistant. "There's no moaning and groaning about how it was done when so-and-so was here. If I want the kids up and running at 6 a.m., they're up and running without all the grumbling."

AN SWC ROMP Arkansas blitzed its way through the SWC season, rampaging to a 13-3 mark, including a 105-82 toasting of No. 24 Texas in Barnhill that vaulted the Razorbacks into the Associated Press poll.

All-SEC selection Keith Wilson had 31 points and Mario Credit added 30 in a game that tied the race at 8-2.

Arkansas went into the final week of the season tied with Texas for the league lead, but the Longhorns faltered while the Razorbacks routed Houston, 107-79,

Reunion Arena became Barnhill South each March.

in their league finale to win the outright title.

"That to me was the beginning of taking Arkansas to the next level," Richardson said. "We were going to win outright championships, we were going to win the league tournament and we were going to go on and do great things in the SWC — and that was with a young team."

BARNHILL SOUTH Richardson's team made good on his boast to take over the 14th annual SWC Classic by ripping through Rice (108-72), Texas A&M (94-84) and Texas (100-76) in the final.

It was an awesome display before a large throng of Razorback fans who once again turned Dallas' Reunion Arena into Barnhill South and inspired *Dallas Times Herald* writer Skip Bayless to pay homage.

"A mere 11,000 of 'em will Winnebago into town for this weekend's SWC Tourney. They'll turn Reunion Arena into "Barnhill South." As in Barnhill Arena, which sells out for every Razorback game. Arkansas fans will fill nearly three-fourths of Reunion. Fans from seven Texas schools may "fill" about half of the remaining one-fourth. That's scary.

Lenzie Howell was named the SWC Tournament MVP after a sterling performance in his hometown.

"Without Arkansas there would be no SWC tourney. Not at a neutral site. The thing would have to be played in the home gym of the SWC winner, where interest was highest. Why not Fayetteville, annually?"

Howell's play was spectacular in his hometown. He grabbed MVP honors and joined Wilson on the all-tournament team while scoring 74 points and pulling down 39 rebounds in three games.

He had 15 points and 15 rebounds against Rice, 31 points and 12 rebounds against A&M and 28 points and 12 rebounds in the win over Texas.

A BASKETBALL TRACK MEET Fifth-seeded Arkansas (24-6) was pitted against Loyola Marymount (20-10) in a first-round NCAA Midwest Regional game in Indianapolis that promised to be a high-scoring matchup.

Arkansas responded by setting an NCAA Midwest Regional record for most points scored in a 120-101 win over the Lions, a game that was 68-53 at halftime.

Mario Credit poured in 34 points in the win while the late Hank Gathers had 28 to lead the losers.

"I knew the game would be in the 100s," Richardson said. "I just hoped we would be the one with the most in the 100s."

NO UALR There was an opportunity for Arkansas' two best college basketball teams to meet in the second round in a game that no doubt would have captured the state's attention even more than the Arkansas-ASU NIT matchup.

Louisville spoiled that scenario by downing UALR, 76-71, thus setting up a second-round matchup with the Razorbacks.

The Cardinals ended the Razorbacks' season, 93-84, as Pervis Ellison had 21 points and 15 rebounds and LaBradford Smith tossed in a game-high 25.

Day had 20, Mayberry 19 and Howell 18 before a crowd of 37,444 in the Hoosier Dome.

1989-90: TO THE FINAL FOUR

This version of Razorbacks (30-5, 14-2) proved to be as high-scoring an outfit as any in school history and that offensive firepower would end up taking them to the Final Four in Denver.

Mayberry was a gifted ballhandler and reluctant shooter on occasions despite his accuracy.

The Razorbacks poured in a school-record 3,345 points — an average of 95.6 points per game — with All-SWC picks Day and Mayberry leading the way.

"That was probably the best of the best offensive teams I have ever had up here," Richardson said. "That

Larry Marks had moments of brilliance for the Razorbacks.

was like a machine. We had so many runs — 10-0, 12-0, 18-0 and we were forcing 25 to 30 turnovers a game. That group had a heck of a knockout punch and not many were left standing when they decided to land it."

That was clear in a pre-conference schedule in which Arkansas scored more than 90 points in nine of its 10 games against non-league foes, including topping the century mark four times.

The topper was a game against U.S. International on Dec. 9. This was a school that had set a record for most points by two teams in a game in a 181-158 loss to Loyola Marymount.

The tiny Florida school, which didn't have a home gym, also had given up 97 points to Oklahoma in an outing right before coming to Fayetteville.

Arkansas joined in on the fun by jumping to a 78-44 lead at halftime and rolled to a 166-101 win with Mayberry pouring in 31 points, Day 24 and Credit 21.

Even in a 101-93 loss at UNLV — which would go on to win the national championship — the Razorbacks displayed offensive fireworks galore. Anderson Hunt led the Rebels with 28 points while Day matched that output for the Razorbacks.

"A lot of people get intimidated (by UNLV), but we decided to just enjoy it," Day said. "The only time we get to see fireworks like this is on the fourth of July."

THE SWC RAMPAGE When Arkansas rallied from 18 down on the road to whip Houston, 82-78, in its SWC-opener, the Razorbacks made a statement to the rest of the league.

By the time the Razorbacks had ripped off an 11-0 league start, the race was over and Arkansas was racing up the Associated Press poll to No. 3.

"During this time I thought we might have a chance to go a long way in the NCAA Tournament," Richardson said. "Maybe not win it all because Vegas had men and everybody else little boys, but then again they had to come from behind to beat us at their place."

Arkansas (20-2, 11-0) did lose a chance to vault to No.1 when Baylor used David Wesley's 23 points to upset the Razorbacks, 82-77, in front of a regional television audience. TCU dealt the stunned frontrunners a second consecutive loss with an 81-79 decision in Fort Worth, but the Razorbacks righted the ship and cruised in with a 14-2 mark and their second consecutive league crown.

They clinched the title outright with a 104-80 victory against Rice in the regular-season finale, in which Sidney Moncrief's jersey was retired.

Day was named the Player of the Year in the SWC while Mayberry was also a first-team selection.

RAZORBACK QUIZ

37. What is the school's all-time record in NIT play?

RAZORBACK QUIZ

38. How many different UA basketball stars have earned All-American status?

Todd Day redefined the off guard position at Arkansas.

STROLLIN' WITH NOLAN The most talked about game in the SWC campaign occurred in Austin, Texas, and featured the Razorbacks and Longhorns in an ABC nationally televised contest.

Arkansas, which had won its first 10 SWC games, looked headed for its first league loss when Mayberry was called for a intentional foul with Texas leading 84-83 with 14 seconds left.

The call gave the Longhorns two free throws and the ball. Richardson rose from his seat and walked past the Texas bench and to his locker room.

"I was feeling sick," Richardson said later. "I was frustrated. I went straight to the bathroom. The officiating was great. It was just great."

Lance Blanks swished two free throws to give the Longhorns an 86-83 lead and Travis Mays was fouled with 11 second left by Ernie Murry.

Mays missed the one-and-one attempt, Oliver Miller rebounded and Mayberry drilled a 25-foot three-pointer to send the game into overtime.

"I'm waiting for this big roar when they beat us and it never came and instead it just got so quiet," Richardson said. "I couldn't figure out what happened, but then our manager came to the door and said 'Coach, let's go. Lee hit a shot and we're in overtime.' I thought about not coming back since they were doing OK without me."

Richardson returned at that point and Arkansas went on to win 103-96 in overtime.

"I told our team that if they take their practice to the floor, they really don't need a coach," Richardson said. "I guess they proved me right. It was the greatest game of my coaching career — bar none."

Texas vehemently protested during the game and afterwards, arguing that Richardson should have gotten a technical for showing up the refs. But ref Mike Tanco disagreed.

"It was during a dead ball and he can leave if he wants to during a dead ball," Tanco said. "He made no gesture to show us up."

NCAA rules spokesman Ed Steitz agreed that Richardson should have been given a technical, but the SWC denied a request by Texas to replay the last 14 seconds of the game.

ANOTHER BANNER POSTSEASON Arkansas ripped through the SWC Classic by pounding SMU (84-61), Baylor (115-75) and Houston (96-84) to advance on to the NCAA Midwest Regional in — of all places — Austin, Texas.

The Razorbacks drew slow-down proponent

Lee Mayberry's 25-foot jumper shocked the Lone Star state.

Ron Huery and Darrell Hawkins celebrate Arkansas' win over Texas that earned the team a berth in the Final Four in Denver.

Princeton in the opening round and barely survived with a 68-64 win, and then edged Dayton, 86-84, to advance to the Midwest Regional finals in Dallas.

The Razorbacks embarrassed North Carolina, 96-73, to set up a matchup with Texas with the winner earning a berth in the Final Four in Denver.

Arkansas had won the last five games between the pair.

"If Texas is in our way," Miller told a Dallas television station, "that's our ticket to the Final Four."

Two free throws by Huery with 15 seconds left put Arkansas up by five in a game it won 88-85. The Razorbacks advanced to their first Final Four in 12 years.

Oliver Miller was the best passing big man the school has ever had.

ROCKY MOUNTAIN HIGH That sent Arkansas off to Denver to join UNLV, Georgia Tech and Duke in the Final Four.

Arkansas led Duke 69-62 with seven minutes left, but seemed to run out of gas in the altitude of Denver. Christian Laettner, who had 19 points and 14 rebounds, led the Blue Devils back despite having four fouls. Duke ended up taking a 97-83 win as Arkansas' sophomore-laden team went cold in the end.

1990-91: A BANNER FOLLOW-UP

Arkansas showed the SWC no mercy while racing to a 15-1 league mark after a article appeared that quoted several SWC coaches as saying the Razorbacks should not be eligible for the title.

This was because the Razorbacks were in their final SWC season and would be headed into the SEC the following season.

"That made me mad," Richardson said. "I had always supported the SWC and the decision was made by higher ups. It was like they just wanted us out of the league so somebody else could win it, really."

The SWC rampage followed a non-conference season in which the Razorbacks made a little history of their own.

They participated in the Dodge Preseason NIT for the first time, whipping Vanderbilt, 107-70, at Barnhill in an opening game and walloping Oklahoma, 110-88, at home as well.

The Razorbacks then avenged their loss to Duke with a 98-88 win in New York's Madison Square Garden before falling to Arizona, 89-77, in the final.

"I thought this was the best team I have ever coached," Richardson said. "From a standpoint of athletic ability, shooting, guarding folks and rebounding."

The non-conference slate also included breaking Missouri's 34-game home winning streak by whipping the Tigers, 95-82, for the first time since the 1980 Great Alaskan Shootout.

#1 VS. #2 The most eagerly anticipated college basketball in recent memory matched up top-ranked and No. 1 UNLV vs. No. 2 Arkansas in a Sunday morning CBS national game.

The Rebels entered the game 19-0 while Arkansas (23-1) was riding a school record 20-game winning streak coming into the contest.

Richardson wouldn't guarantee a victory, but felt pretty good about his team's chances.

NFL great Walter Peyton and Major League Baseball star Andy Van Slyke were among those who saw the Razorbacks take a 50-46 lead into halftime.

UNLV showed its poise by coming out and ripping off 16 of the second half's first 18 points and eventually grabbing a 22-point lead before winning, 112-105.

Stacy Augmon had 31 points to lead UNLV, Hunt 26 and Larry Johnson 25 for the Rebels while Day had 26 and Miller 22 for Arkansas.

THE DORM INCIDENT No. 5 Arkansas clinched its third straight outright SWC title by ripping Baylor, 106-74, at Barnhill, leaving them 15-0 in the league and with a chance to become the first team since the 1976-77 Razorbacks to go unbeaten in league play.

The Razorbacks' SWC finale was at Texas, a game that got lost in controversy that led up to it.

Several UA players were investigated for an alleged sexual incident that occurred in the dorm, but no charges

Former San Jacinto Junior College standouts Larry Johnson and Butch Morris were matched up in the much-anticipated UA-UNLV game.

were filed. Still the incident drew protests from women's groups and was the subject of vast media attention.

"As coach of this University I am naturally concerned when there are allegations and misconduct on the part of my team members," Richardson said. "But I let the authorities conduct their investigation before I take any action. Then I make my part of it."

Richardson suspended one player and three others were disciplined by the University's Judicial Board after the season.

All this took a toll on the Razorbacks, who lost to Texas, 99-86, in Austin, but they regrouped quickly.

Arkansas' 1990-91 team had a chance to match the 1976-77 Razorbacks' perfect conference mark, but lost at Texas.

ANOTHER FINAL FOUR? After an absolute picnic at the SWC Classic in which the Razorbacks routed Texas A&M (108-61), Rice (109-80) and Texas (120-89), Richardson's squad set its sights on a second straight trip to the Final Four.

The Razorbacks started their quest by leveling Georgia State (117-76) and Arizona State (97-90) in the NCAA Southeast Regional in Atlanta.

Arkansas then downed Alabama, 93-70, to move within one win of a return trip and raced to a 12-point halftime lead over Kansas in the regional final.

The Razorbacks have been in the NCAA Tournament in all but Nolan Richardson's first two seasons.

But the Jayhawks rallied for a 93-81 win to end the Razorbacks' season as Alonzo Jamison poured in a career-high 26 points for the Jayhawks.

Day scored 26 points, which gave him 786 for a season, a new single-season record for Arkansas (34-4).

1991-92: NEW LEAGUE, ANOTHER TITLE

Although Arkansas started the season without All-American Todd Day and three other players, the Razorbacks still ended up making their first year in the SEC another title-laden campaign.

"Going into the SEC changes a lot of things for us," Richardson said. "During the last three years we dominated the SWC. If we were in the SWC this year, we would be disappointed to lose more than a game. Even I would pick us to win again. But it's a whole new game in the SEC."

MISSING DAY Day, who couldn't play until Jan. 2 because of the dorm incident and allegations of cheating on a test, did show he was ready to have a big year by scoring 42 points in a Red-White game before the season.

It was clear the Razorbacks missed that scoring output in a 87-76 loss to visiting Missouri, but they did

Nolan Richardson counsels Todd Day during a break in the action.

race out to a 12-1 record without him.

Day returned in Arkansas' final non-conference against Quincy College and pumped in 26 points in just 22 minutes as the No. 16 Razorbacks rolled to a 123-60 win in Pine Bluff.

THE SEC ARRIVES Arkansas made a grand entrance into the SEC by blasting Auburn, 110-91, before 9,468 fans at Barnhill Arena.

Day had 35 points as the Razorbacks ran wild to a 57-30 halftime lead.

"In the first half, and I've been coaching for sometime," Richardson said, "I saw one of the finest exhibitions of fastbreak, three-point shooting, defense, tough tenacious rebounding and guys that are making excellent passes that I have seen since I have been here."

Arkansas, which lost its second game to Alabama, raced out to a 5-1 league mark. That included a 101-90 victory at LSU, in which Day scored a career-high 43

Arkansas has won or shared the SEC West Divisional title in four of its five seasons in the league.

points and LSU's Shaquille O'Neal had 27 points and 16 rebounds.

Next was a showdown in Lexington with Kentucky, the league's premier team, before a Rupp Arena record-crowd of 24,324 fans.

Mayberry's 23 points led six Razorbacks (17-3, 6-1) in double figures as Arkansas ran over the Wildcats, 105-88, to break a 21-game home winning streak under coach Rick Pitino.

"We had to come in and prove something," UA center Oliver Miller said. "We played good offense, good defense and did the things it takes to win. We are not cocky, we just feel that when we play our game we can beat any team even on their floor — and that is just what we did."

Arkansas wrapped up the SEC Western Division and overall title by downing LSU, 106-92 in overtime, March 4 at Barnhill Arena.

THE SEC TOURNAMENT While Arkansas fans couldn't get the amount of tickets they were use to having at the SWC Classic, they nevertheless made their presence known at their first SEC event in Birmingham.

Meanwhile, on the court the Razorbacks split a pair of exciting games. Arkansas beat Georgia, 73-60, in an opening-round game to set up a semifinal with Alabama, a rubber game between the two squads that had split during the season.

Arkansas appeared to be close to putting the game away when Roosevelt Wallace stepped to the free-throw line with the Razorbacks leading 89-87 with 23.8 second left.

But Wallace missed and with future NBA players James Robinson, Robert Horry and Latrell Spreewell bottled up, Eliott Washington buried a three-pointer with two seconds left to give Alabama a 90-89 victory.

"No doubt in my mind that our three games with Arkansas this season were some of the greatest games I have ever been associated with," Alabama coach Wimp Sanderson said. "This has to be one of the greatest games in SEC Tournament history."

AN OLD FRIEND The NCAA brackets found Arkansas off to Milwaukee to meet an old friend in Scott Edgar, a former Razorback assistant who had taken his first Murray State team to the Big Dance.

His staff included Kenneth "Boo" Roth, a former Arkansas graduate assistant. A Lexington paper had dubbed their team the "Racerbacks."

"He (Richardson) would lose respect for me if I didn't do everything I could to win," Edgar said. "Once the ball is tossed up, that midcourt separates enemies and allies."

Arkansas raced away from a 57-57 tie with 10:17 left

Scott Edgar was once a trusted Richardson aide who found himself matched up with his former boss in the NCAA Tournament.

to an 11-point lead with just more than four minutes left in a game the Razorbacks ended up winning, 80-69.

Arkansas' season ended just a game later when Memphis State freshman David Vaughn scored off his own miss as time expired to lift his team to a 82-80 win and end the college careers of Day, Mayberry and Miller.

"Sometimes maybe it is not in the cards for you to win a basketball game," Richardson said.

1992-93: A NEW ERA

With Day, Mayberry, Miller and Morris all playing in the NBA, it was a fact the Razorback squad would face a rebuilding year.

Their prospects dimmed when top recruit Corliss Williamson of Russellville broke a bone in his foot in September and missed the first part of the season.

But blessed with a team the coach called "Richardson's Runts," Arkansas nevertheless powered its way to a 22-9 finish and an unexpected berth in the Sweet 16.

"Everybody thought that when the Days and the Mayberrys and the Millers went out the door, it would be a long time before we would be back," Richardson said. "But it turned out that instead of rebuilding, we just reloaded."

Corliss Williamson was viewed as the state's best high school basketball player throughout his three-year prep career.

THURMAN COMES ALIVE Scotty Thurman, a 6-foot-5 forward from Ruston, La., who was overlooked by LSU until Richardson had already signed him, put the Razorbacks on his back early on in the 1992-93 campaign.

He had only five points in a 81-76 upset of No. 8 Memphis State in Barnhill in the season-opener, but then heated up in a season in which he would be tabbed All-SEC.

Thurman pumped in 23 of his game-high 28 points in the second half, Warren Linn added 15 and Robert Shepherd recorded a school-record nine steals as Arkansas shocked Arizona, 86-80.

Arizona had won 79 of its past 80 games at the McKale Center before the young Razorbacks arrived.

"I've been around 29 years and won some big games, but this is probably one of the — if not the biggest — I've ever had and we beat Kentucky at Kentucky last year," Richardson said. "The difference is I had a squad to beat Kentucky. I didn't know if we had a squad to come beat Arizona."

Thurman, showing an uncanny touch from three-point range, then poured in a career-high 34 points as Arkansas won at Missouri, 73-68, in a battle of unbeatens.

Thurman hit 7 of 11 from three-point range as the Razorbacks snapped Missouri's 16-game homecourt

Warren Linn's finest hour was a 15-point performance in the upset at Arizona.

Scotty Thurman was a standout for the Razorbacks from the time he stepped on the campus as a freshman.

winning streak and kept Tigers coach Norm Stewart from getting his 500th win.

ANOTHER TITLE Arkansas, which got Williamson on board for the conference season, would finish only 10-6 in the SEC Western Division standings, but that was good enough to claim a divisional title in a balanced race.

The biggest of all those wins was clearly a 101-94 win over Kentucky in Barnhill Arena.

Kentucky coach Rick Pitino laughed when he was greeted by the theme from "The Godfather" upon his arrival, but found nothing funny in the performance of Williamson.

Williamson, outshining Kentucky All-American Jamal Mashburn, poured in 22 points to lead his team to the win.

The Razorbacks' most impressive SEC win was an 115-58 flogging of Mississippi State in Fayetteville 10 days later. The Bulldogs had edged Arkansas, 80-76, earlier that season in Starkville.

Arkansas again topped Georgia, 65-60, in SEC Tournament play at Lexington before Kentucky eliminated the Razorbacks with a 92-81 win on its home floor.

The Wildcats jumped to a 17-0 lead only to see Arkansas cut that deficit to two before the game was over.

"It's not very often that a university would have to replace (four NBA draft picks) with these young kids, come to this point, have an opportunity to be so far down and be able to come back," Richardson said.

THE NCAA SURPRISE Darrell Hawkins' NCAA Tournament-record eight steals tells all anyone needed to know about Arkansas' 94-64 flogging of Holy Cross in an NCAA East Regional first-round game at Winston-Salem, N.C.

The Crusaders were unable to handle Arkansas' press and suffered 31 turnovers.

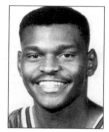

Darrell Hawkins was a leader to "Richardson's Runts."

The Razorbacks then had to rally from 10 down to whip St. John's, 80-74, and advance on to a face top-seeded North Carolina in the Sweet 16.

Despite having to use the 6-7 Williamson to guard North Carolina's 7-0 Eric Montross, Arkansas used its quickness to stun the Tar Heels, who had won their second-round game by 45 points.

The game was tied 69-69 with 6:25 left and trailed just 75-74 with 1:05 remaining in the game. But eventual national champion North Carolina made enough big plays down the stretch to pull out an 80-74 win.

It was a game that Arkansas (22-9) thought it should have won.

"What it did was tell our kids they could play with anybody," Richardson said. "We knew with two 6-11 freshman centers coming in and almost everybody coming back, we really had a chance to win it all next season."

The Magic Years

No time in Razorback basketball history has been more magical than the 1993-94 and 1994-95 seasons, when the Arkansas program made back-to-back appearances in the NCAA championship game.

If there was any doubt that Arkansas belonged among the elite of college basketball, those two seasons erased any doubt.

"Before when you thought of the Top 20 college basketball programs in the nation, you thought of Arkansas," Richardson said. "But now when you want to narrow it down to just a handful and you talk about the Kentuckys, the North Carolinas, the Dukes and Kansas, you have to put the winningest college basketball program of the 1990s right in there — the Arkansas Razorbacks."

Arkansas' 1994 national championship made for banner headlines in the newspapers around the state and nation.

1993-94: NATIONAL CHAMPS

Richardson knew his team would be better in 1993-94 because it had added two Parade All-American high school centers in 6-foot-11 Darnell Robinson, a gifted offensive force, and 6-11 Lee Wilson, a defensive presence in the paint.

They also had added a three-point bomber in junior college scoring sensation Alex Dillard, a 25-year-old nicknamed "The Old Man" whose range was anywhere inside the city limits.

The Arkansas starting lineup of 6-5 Scotty Thurman, 6-7 Corliss Williamson, 6-2 Corey Beck, 6-9 Dwight Stewart and 6-4 Clint McDaniel was bolstered by a strong bench that included 6-4 Roger Crawford, Dillard, Wilson, Robinson, 6-7 Davor Rimac, 6-8 Ray Biggers, 6-7 senior Ken Biley and walk-ons John Engskov and Reggie Merritt.

The team was also bolstered by the excitement of Bud Walton Arena, a new $36 million dollar palace that would allow the team to play before a home crowd of 20,000 fans per game.

"I knew we had the chance to be good — really good," Richardson said. "We now had great outside shooting, height and physical presence and most importantly a desire to do anything it took to win. This team absolutely hated losing and would do anything — bite, scratch and claw — to make sure it didn't."

40 MINUTES OF HELL

40 MINUTES OF HELL For many years, Arkansas' pressure defense had been intertwined with the phrase "40 minutes of Hell."

But Richardson has long pointed out that the phrase really was coined to describe his first 40 minutes of practice, in which his team puts in its hardest work.

"From the first day, I knew no one was going to outwork us," Richardson said. "I knew no one was going to lay it on the line and give it everything they had as much as this team would. I was right."

Roger Crawford was one of only two seniors on Arkansas' national championship squad.

Lee Wilson (left) and Corey Beck (right) show LSU guard Jamie Brandon what 40 minutes of Hell is all about.

THE OPENER The Razorbacks, who moved up to No. 2 in the Associated Press poll before the start of the contest, ripped out to a 13-0 lead and went on to a 93-67 rout over Murray State.

Crawford and Williamson both had 13 points to lead a balanced Razorback attack before a crowd of 20,048 that watched Arkansas force 27 turnovers.

"I hate to say it," Murray State coach Scott Edgar noted, "but their big people were out-running our guards down the court. Their second team might be 20 points better than anybody in the Ohio Valley."

A PERFECT GAME There was not a lot of differences in the basketball teams at Missouri and Arkansas in 1993-94. Both of them advanced to the Elite Eight and both won their conferences going away.

But there was a tremendous difference in the pair on Dec. 2, 1993 — a 52-point difference to be exact.

Thurman's 18 points led seven Razorbacks in double figures as Arkansas humbled Missouri, 120-68, in front of a ESPN national audience and a stunned Richardson and Tiger coach Norm Stewart. The Razorbacks hit 16 of 25 three-pointers while shooting 59 percent from the field overall.

"Norm told me after the game that he felt sorry for me," Richardson said. "I knew what he meant. People would now be expecting us to win by that much every night. We were good, but nobody is that good. But everything was just perfect. We could have kicked the ball and it would have gone in tonight."

THE DECEMBER ROLL Arkansas continued to pound its opponents home and away in December, including a 96-78 road win over old rival Memphis State that came just 48 hours after the Razorbacks were named No. 1.

Dillard began to make his presence felt, especially when he pumped in an incredible 13 three-pointers in a 39-point performance that led to a 57-point rout of Delaware State.

"Awesome," Delaware State coach Jeff Jones exclaimed. "No other word can describe them. They have everything it takes. I've seen Kentucky, North Carolina and Indiana play and they are a step above those teams. They are awesome."

THE PREZ ARRIVES Before Dec. 28, 1993, no sitting President of the United States has ever attended a college basketball game.

But long-time Razorback fan Bill Clinton took the opportunity to visit Fayetteville to catch the Razorbacks' 129-63 thrashing of Texas Southern in a game in which

RAZORBACK QUIZ

42. Who was Arkansas' athletic director before Frank Broyles?

RAZORBACK QUIZ

43. What statewide televised victory is generally regarded as the contest which brought Arkansas basketball fans around?

Corliss Williamson visits with President Clinton in the Arkansas locker room.

the home team tossed in a mind-boggling 20 three-pointers.

"The President just blew my mind," Williamson said. "It's not every day someone gets to meet and shake hands with the President. This is something that I can tell my grandkids."

THE SEC SEASON BEGINS SLOWLY Arkansas handily defeated Ole Miss in its SEC-opener, 87-61, but fell from its lofty No. 1 perch just a game later when it hit the road with its glistening 10-0 mark.

When Clint McDaniel missed a jumper with 10 seconds left and Dwight Stewart's putback failed as well, the Crimson Tide celebrated a 66-64 decision like it was a national championship win.

Arkansas then slipped by LSU (84-83) at home and Auburn (117-105) on the road before hitting its second speed bump in the road.

Mississippi State (5-0) took control of the SEC West race with a 72-71 win over Arkansas (3-2) that left the

Known as the Big Dog, Dwight Stewart redefined the role of being a big man at Arkansas with his outside touch.

Razorbacks not only not No. 1 in the country, but not even No. 1 in their own division.

It would be the last time that Arkansas would experience defeat in the regular season.

"We found ourselves looking up and decided to go to work," Richardson said. "You might say we brought our lunch with us and put in a full day's work every day for the rest of the season."

OWNING THE WILDCATS It appeared that Arkansas' regular-season mastery of Kentucky might be coming to an end when the Wildcats jumped to a 39-24 lead with 4:44 left in the first half.

But it was at that point that Kentucky sophomore forward Rodrick Rhodes felt the need to gyrate and taunt the Razorbacks after a Gimel Martinez three-pointer. What he did was simply get a technical and infuriate his

Arkansas has won three of its four regular season matchups with Kentucky since joining the SEC.

Arkansas marched into Kentucky and left the Bluegrass State in shock with a comeback win.

coach and the Arkansas players.

The Razorbacks closed within 41-36 by half and then sprinted away in the second half when Thurman contributed 20 of his game-high 26 points.

Williamson added 21 points and 14 rebounds in the second straight win for Arkansas in Rupp Arena and the Razorbacks' third regular-season win in a row over the Wildcats.

"My congratulations to Arkansas," Kentucky coach Rick Pitino said. "They've done this to us twice in a row. They've been a superior basketball team twice in a row. … This is the most disappointed I've ever been in a team in my 20 years of coaching. It (Rhodes' technical) is too stupid to even talk about. We showed more childishness tonight in every facet of the game. In the second half, we folded our tent and went home."

Alex Dillard set a school record with 13 three-pointers in a single game.

OWNING LSU Arkansas then cruised through the rest of its 14-2 SEC campaign with only one game in doubt in the final minutes.

That was a game at LSU, where the Razorbacks found themselves down 93-90 with 10 seconds left and Tiger guard Andre Owens standing on the free-throw line with a chance to ice the game.

Instead, he missed the front end of a one-and-one attempt and Dillard faked out two defenders before burying a three-pointer at the buzzer to send the game into overtime.

Arkansas would go on to win, 108-105, in a game in which Thurman, not recruited by LSU head coach Dale

The Razorbacks have owned LSU since joining the SEC, but the games have not been easy.

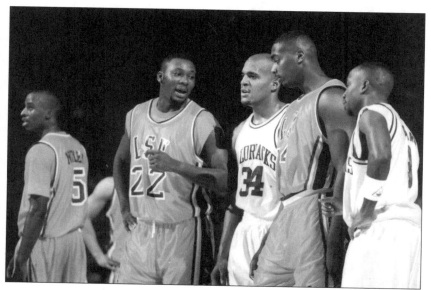

Brown, had 27 points. It was the sixth straight Razorback win over the Tigers.

"I have never felt more pain for a team than this one," Brown said. "I'm so proud of them. Arkansas is the best team in the country. They made some impossible shots."

Beck takes a charge from Georgetown's Robert Churchwell during the NCAA title run.

A SHORT STAY IN MEMPHIS Riding a 12-game winning streak into The Pyramid in Memphis, Arkansas continued its three-year SEC Tournament tradition by eliminating Georgia, 95-83, in a quarterfinal matchup.

But the Razorbacks left the Bluff City a day later when a hot-shooting Kentucky team prevailed, 90-78, despite 23 points and 16 rebounds from Williamson.

"We stunk the whole gym up," Beck said. "We've got to regroup and play great in the NCAA Tournament."

THE RUN BEGINS Arkansas was one of four NCAA No. 1 seeds that lost in its conference tournament but came back strong to make waves in the NCAA.

It began with a first-round matchup in the Midwest Regional in Oklahoma City against 16th-seeded North Carolina A&T, a 16-13 squad that nevertheless trailed by only four points with nine minutes remaining in the game.

Beck's defense took charge and a 7-0 run led to a 94-79 victory in which Williamson led the way with 24 points and Thurman added 19.

That set up a second-round game with Georgetown that turned into a wrestling match in the second half.

When McDaniel and Georgetown guard Robert Churchwell became entangled underneath the Arkansas basket, both Thurman and Hoya Don Reid raced from the bench for support.

All that did was get Thurman and Reid tossed, ejections that reduced the firepower of the Arkansas offense and the effectiveness of the Georgetown defense.

Arkansas, which lost Crawford with an injury for the rest of the season, went big at that point by inserting Williamson, Robinson, Wilson and Stewart at the same time and overpowered the Hoyas, 85-73.

GLAMOUR GAME After Williamson and McDaniel had 21 points each in dispatching Tulsa, 103-84, in a relatively easy Sweet 16 round contest in Dallas, it set the stage for a matchup between two of the most highly-regarded teams of the 1990s.

The Razorbacks (28-3) and Michigan (24-7), both featuring plenty of swagger and the trend-setting baggiest shorts of any two teams in America, met for a berth in the Final Four with President Clinton once more in attendance.

A Michigan win would mean a third straight trip to the Final Four for the Fab Five — minus one since Chris Webber had gone pro before the season.

"I respect what they have done, but we are planning on taking matters into our own hands this time," Thurman said. "We feel we are the best team in America and deserve to be where we are."

The Razorbacks backed that up with a 76-68 win that punched them a ticket to Charlotte, N.C., for the college basketball showdown.

Juwan Howard had a game-high 30 points for

RAZORBACK QUIZ

44. Who was the school's first 7-footer?

An offensive force in high school, Clint McDaniel became a defensive stopper at Arkansas.

RAZORBACK QUIZ

45. How many rebounds did the Razorbacks have against Fort Chaffee in 1956?

BUD WALTON ARENA

The Arkansas basketball program continued to grow in popularity and national stature when Nolan Richardson came aboard.

When Arkansas joined the SEC, it was clear that its facilities were not up to league standards. One man who helped fix that was J.L. "Bud" Walton, one of the founders of the Wal-Mart empire.

Walton dropped by Athletic Director Frank Broyles' office one day. After a few minutes of chatting about bird hunting, Walton posed a question for Broyles.

"He said 'Do you still think you can build a competitive arena for $30,000,000?' " Broyles related. "I said 'Yes I do.' And he said 'Well count on me for half of it. Goodbye. I'm going bird hunting' and walked out."

Richardson was overwhelmed by Walton's gifts, which enabled the University to build an arena that seats 19,200 and is perpetually soldout.

"I already had a tremendous respect for Bud and Sam Walton, who were two great sources of inspiration for anyone who was trying to succeed," Richardson said. "They had already done so much for the university both academically and athletically with their generosity. But when Mr. Walton made his incredibly generous offer, I was humbled beyond belief. I could see the advantages it would bring us and knew the dream of winning a national championship was much closer to becoming a reality."

Arkansas christened its new building in 1993-94 with a dream season that started with a 93-67 win over Murray State and culminated in a national championship.

As Arkansas was capping a 31-3

The late Bud Walton (right) and his family have been long-time Razorback supporters.

season with a win over Duke in the national championship, its loyal fans packed inside Bud Walton Arena to watch the game on big screen televisions.

"By the end of the year we found out that at least 90,000 different people had been able to come to at least one game in our new arena," said Broyles, who kept back some season tickets and split them into three game packages so more people could get in.

A look at the outside of Bud Walton Arena on a rare off night during the winter.

Arkansas has continued to be hard to beat at Bud Walton Arena since it opened in November of 1993.

Arkansas' Alex Dillard and Michigan's Jimmy King were two of the players in a glamour matchup between two of the nation's top programs.

Michigan while Thurman led the Razorbacks with 20.

It capped a great day for Richardson, who was named the Naismith Coach of the Year in the morning.

"I can say this," Richardson said. "Never had I had all these things happen in one day — Coach of the Year, the President comes to the game and hugs you and you win a trip to the Final Four."

RAZING ARIZONA Arkansas arrived amidst the usual hoopla of the Final Four, but with a coach who knew how to help his team stay focused on the job at hand.

That was primarily slowing down Arizona guards Kahlid Reeves and Damon Stoudamire in a semifinal matchup against the Wildcats.

"All I've been hearing about them is they can't be stopped," Beck said. "All I know is that they are very good players, but we did a pretty good job on them last season."

That was during an 86-80 upset win at Arizona in which the pair was held to 16 points.

Reeves and Stoudamire didn't fair much better on April 2, 1994, when Arkansas' guards hounded them into a combined 11-of-43 outing from the field.

Williamson had 29 points, grabbed 13 rebounds and had five assists and helped lead his team back after

Corey Beck and his teammates shut down and shut up Arizona's backcourt.

Arizona took a 67-62 lead with 8:02 left in the game.

It was at that point that the Wildcats "hit the wall."

"We had to go for the jugular at that point," Richardson said. "We had no choice. Even when they were getting the lead you could see Arizona's legs getting tired. I told our players everybody has been waiting for '40 minutes of Hell' and we are going to give it to them. Or at least eight minutes of torture."

Arkansas turned up the pressure on its pressure defense, ripped off a 12-0 scoring run and never trailed again in racing away to a 91-82 win and a trip to the championship game.

"This is what coaches and players work for all their lives," Richardson said. "A chance to be in the final game. A chance to win it all."

DUKE-ING IT OUT FOR RESPECT
When you play in the NCAA championship game, you could care less where it is played.

That's why Richardson didn't mind at all that his chance for a national title was to be played in Duke's backyard.

Arkansas coach Nolan Richardson started little-used Ken Biley against Grant Hill and the Duke Blue Devils in the NCAA championship game.

Coach Nolan Richardson and players like Corliss Williamson (shown here) proved that Arkansas was a pretty smart team afterall.

"Anytime you can come in and beat somebody in their backyard, that's sweeter than any juice you can drink," Richardson said. "When you go to the backyard of the smartest team in America and win, that's super-sweet."

All season long Richardson and his team had believed that they were not getting enough respect and continued that mantra at the press conference the day before.

He was incensed that a Detroit sportswriter smugly

predicted that "the smarter team will win and the smart team is Duke."

Richardson made a grand gesture by starting senior Ken Biley, who had not played much during the season. Biley defended Duke star Grant Hill and held him scoreless in the three minutes he played. Hill would go on to score just half of his average of 24 points.

Duke's 13-0 run during the middle of the game gave the Blue Devils a 48-38 lead with 17:09 left, but the Razorbacks steadied themselves and began a comeback as Duke began to show fatigue.

"We used a lot of emotion in that run," Duke coach Mike Krzyzewski said. "And they wore us down in the second half."

The game came down to Thurman's three-pointer from the right side with the shot clock running out and the game tied 70-70. Dwight Stewart fumbled the ball before hitting Thurman, who just got the shot off over the outstretched hands of Antonio Lang.

The shot hit nothing but net to put Arkansas up 73-70 with 50.9 seconds left. After Duke's Chris Collins

Nolan Richardson rewarded Ken Biley's years of hard work with a start in the NCAA championship game.

Nolan Richardson had the last laugh on his critics in 1993-94.

Corliss Williamson led the Razorbacks to glory.

Walk-on John Engskov was on a team that played before the President and won a national title.

missed a 25-footer that would have tied it, the Razorbacks started a march to the free-throw line that would result in a 76-72 win.

Williamson had 23 points, Thurman 15 points and Beck 15 points and 10 rebounds for Arkansas (31-3) in the win.

"It was the greatest game in the history of the University of Arkansas," Richardson said. "I want to thank Frank Broyles for sticking his neck out and hiring me and giving me a chance to bring the national championship to Arkansas."

Right after the win, Richardson pointed to the sky in remembrance of daughter Yvonne.

"Baby we've won you another one," Richardson said. "Not just another one. The big one."

1994-95: NOT A BAD ENCORE

With everyone except Ken Biley coming back, it was no wonder that many people were asking Arkansas' players if they could become the first group since Indiana in 1976 to go undefeated.

Those questions went by the wayside as soon as the season opened against Massachusetts in the Hall of Fame game at Springfield, Mass.

The question became moot as Lou Roe poured in a game-high 34 points and grabbed 13 rebounds as UMass humbled No. 1 Arkansas, 104-80, before what amounted to a home crowd for the Minutemen.

Thurman had 17 points and McDaniel 16 while Williamson was held to 15 points and seven rebounds.

"They came to play with a very good, aggressive basketball game," Richardson said. "They should be commended for their effort and how hard they worked. We talked about how each team will come after you like it is a national championship game. We did not as a team accept the challenge."

Walk-on Reggie Meritt enjoyed the chance to work with the likes of Todd Day and Corliss Williamson.

RIGHTING THE SHIP Thoroughly embarrassed, Arkansas rebounded two days later by whipping No. 14 Georgetown, 97-79, in the opening game of the

Clint McDaniel applies defense against Arkansas native Wes Flanigan in a game with Auburn.

inaugural Martin Luther King Classic in Memphis.

The Razorbacks led by as much as 32 in a game that featured the debut of Hoya recruit Allen Iverson.

"I don't know if we were angry, but we were certainly embarrassed," Richardson said.

HAWAIIAN DOMINANCE No. 3 Arkansas was rolling once it got to the islands for the 31st annual Kraft Rainbow Classic riding an eight-game winning streak and all but forgetting about its humbling opener.

The Razorbacks dispatched Cincinnati and slipped by Oklahoma to advance to the championship game against Iowa.

Williamson, the tournament MVP, Beck and Thurman all had 17 points as Arkansas whipped the Hawkeyes, 101-92, before 10,031 at the University of Hawaii's new Special Events Center.

"When we came to this tournament, we talked about how the Razorbacks had not won an in-season tournament since 1968," Richardson said. "So for the kids to be seniors and have won the national championship and in the same year win the Rainbow Classic is something they will never forget."

SLOW SEC START, STRONG ENDING Ole Miss upset a tired Razorback team, 76-61, just two days after Arkansas made the long flight back from Hawaii.

It was an eye-opening SEC-opener for the Razorbacks, who nevertheless rebounded to post a 12-4 mark that tied them for first in the SEC West with Mississippi State.

The SEC season was highlighted by a 94-92 win over Kentucky at Barnhill Arena in a game played before a packed Bud Walton Arena and a national television audience on Super Sunday.

Williamson — sporting a new hairdo he called the nasty streak — had a season-high 28 points and Thurman buried an 18-footer with 8.2 seconds left to cap off his 22-point effort. Tony Delk had 31 to lead Kentucky, which lost its chance to win when McDaniel stripped Jeff Sheppard.

"It was like a heavyweight championship bout," Richardson said. "No one wanted to go down. It's too bad somebody had to win, but I'm glad it was us. It was a great, great college basketball game. Possibly the best of all-time."

The low point was a 79-74 loss to Alabama in Bud Walton Arena, the first Razorback loss in Bud Walton Arena.

"I told our team long you live, die you must," Richardson said.

RAZORBACK QUIZ

46. What is the school's all-time record in NCAA competition?

RAZORBACK QUIZ

47. How many of the Razorbacks' nine coaches have won conference championships?

THE SEC TOURNAMENT Arkansas eliminated Vanderbilt and Alabama in the SEC Tournament in Atlanta before playing yet another classic in the final against Kentucky.

The Wildcats rallied from 19 down only to see Rodrick Rhodes miss two free throws with 1.3 seconds left in regulation that could have won it.

Arkansas jumped out to a nine-point overtime lead with 1:38 left in the extra frame, but Kentucky rallied for a 94-92 win that gave coach Rick Pitino a 12-0 mark in the tournament.

Williamson roars in for a dunk against Syracuse during the 1995 NCAA Tournament.

48. Arkansas has the most victories over which school?

Thurman and Williamson visit with the media at the 1995 NCAA Final Four in Seattle.

BACK TO THE FUTURE Arkansas' 1994-95 NCAA run was certainly much more problematic than its sprint through the tournament the season before.

The No. 6 Razorbacks (27-6) edged Texas Southern, 79-78, in the first round of the NCAA Midwest Regional in Austin, a place Richardson and his Razorbacks were booed incessantly by University of Texas fans.

In the second game of the tourney, Arkansas' season appeared to be coming to an end when Syracuse, in the lead, came up with a loose ball with just seconds left, but Lawrence Moten called a timeout his team didn't have and allowed Arkansas to tie up the game. Thurman and Dillard then buried deep three-pointers in overtime to send Arkansas to the win, 96-94.

"Once again we found a way to win," Richardson said. "It amazes me that our kids just never quit."

Arkansas then edged Memphis, 69-61 in overtime, in the Sweet 16 in Kansas City after Corey Beck hit a game-tying free throw with 11.5 seconds to put the game into overtime.

The Razorbacks then punched their ticket to the Final Four in Seattle with a 68-61 win over Virginia in the Regional final.

SLEEPLESS IN SEATTLE A Final Four of Arkansas, North Carolina, UCLA and Oklahoma State not only brought three of college basketball's titans to Seattle, but the two

Williamson and North Carolina's Rasheed Wallace were matched up in a Final Four semifinal.

coaches who had led the Razorbacks to their greatest success.

Many envisioned a championship matchup featuring Richardson and OSU's Eddie Sutton, but only Richardson's team made it through to the finals as UCLA ousted the Cowboys, 74-61.

Arkansas held up its end of the bargain by downing North Carolina, 75-68, before 38,540 fans in the Kingdome.

Williamson had 19 of his 21 points in the second half while Stewart added 15 and McDaniel hit four free throws in the last 27.5 seconds to seal the win.

North Carolina All-American Jerry Stackhouse had 18 points but missed a free throw that would have tied the game with 47 second left. His fatigue showed as did his whole team's in a stretch where the Razorback defense didn't allow a field goal for more than 12 minutes.

"I told our kids that deep inside and in our hearts we know as individuals that we have had a phenomenal season," Richardson said. "We've taken everybody's best shot — everybody's. And we are still ticking. We've got one game to go and let's hope we end the fairy tale story."

UCLA's Ed O'Bannon was named the MVP of the Final Four, just as Williamson had been a season before.

UCLA REIGNS Back-to-back championships for Arkansas was not in the plans for UCLA senior Ed O'Bannon, who turned up his game when teammate Tyus Edney was unable to play due to injury.

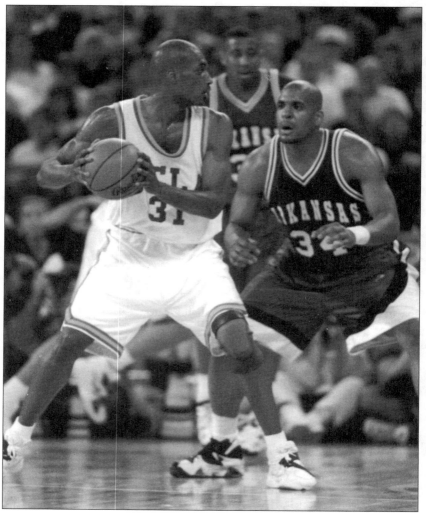

O'Bannon had 30 points and 17 rebounds and Toby Bailey added 26 as the Bruins won their 11th national championship and first in 20 years by downing Arkansas, 89-78.

"As I told them, 32 times we were very happy and seven times we were very sad," Richardson said. "It just so happened that the last one made us the saddest. But you have to remember there were 304 teams that wanted to be where they were tonight."

1995-96: A REBUILDING YEAR

Eight seniors out the door and Williamson and Thurman declaring for the NBA draft left Richardson with practically a whole new team.

His lone experience was in the form of Robinson and Wilson and lightly-used Landis Williams. The Razorbacks ended the season starting four freshmen.

He also suffered a jolt in February when leading scorer Jesse Pate and leading rebounder Sunday Adebayo were declared ineligible because of a certification error.

It would be a year in which Arkansas would drop out of the Associated Press Top 25 for the first time in 53 polls, but get better as the year went on.

"It was a year when we started teaching and everything began to take toward the end of the year," Richardson said. "They came so far."

BIG WINS The Razorbacks (22-13) did have some big wins in 1995-96 with no regular-season win any more

RAZORBACK QUIZ

49. The Razorbacks' title at the Rainbow Classic in Hawaii in 1995 was the first in-season tournament title since when?

Nolan Richardson and wife Rose hug after a win.

impressive than a matchup with Missouri.

It came just one day after Robinson suffered his third broken bone in his foot in as many years, an ailment that would sideline him for 13 games.

Arkansas responded by blasting Missouri, 104-93, before the ESPN cameras in a game in which the Razorbacks blocked a school- and SEC-record 18 shots.

Every Razorback home game since 1977-78 has been a sell-out.

The Razorbacks finished 9-7 in the SEC, a mark that tied them for second in the Western Division with Alabama.

They were able to clinch that spot by rallying from 17 down at LSU to win 94-79 as freshman guard Pat Bradley pumped in 25 points and freshman guard Kareem Reid had a UA school-record 14 assists.

SWEET, SWEET 16 There was a lot of debate over whether Arkansas even deserved to be in the NCAA tournament

Richardson, shown here with CBS sportscaster Billy Packer, returned all but one player from his national championship team for the 1994-95 campaign.

and the seeds indicated that the Razorbacks were given one of the last at-large berths.

That berth was probably clinched in one of their finest efforts of the season, an 80-58 thrashing of South Carolina in the quarterfinal round of the SEC Tournament.

But the 12th-seeded Razorbacks made their mark once they arrived at the NCAA East Regional in Providence, R.I., by eliminating fourth-seeded Penn State, 86-80, and fifth-seeded Marquette, 65-56.

The success was due in large part to a return to the 40 minutes of Hell pressing defense, which Richardson decided his young charges were not ready for earlier in the season.

"I thought our pressure defense was the key to our two victories up here," Richardson said. "This team plays defense in a different way and it is difficult for teams to adjust in a one-game shot."

The run ended in the Sweet 16 in Atlanta when No. 1 UMass whipped cold-shooting Arkansas, 79-63.

"They (the Minutemen) played one of their great games this season," Richardson said. "But I'm proud of our kids. I told them they were overachievers. I've never had a group that worked this hard."

RAZORBACK QUIZ

50. What was Nolan Richardson's record at Western Texas Junior College?

By the Numbers

The statistics found here are provided by the University of Arkansas Sports Information department and are updated through the 1995-96 school year.

SEASON-BY-SEASON SUMMARY

Year	Coach	Overall	Conf.	Year	Coach	Overall	Conf.
1923	Francis Schmidt	17-11	3-9	1960	Glen Rose	16-7	9-5
1924	Francis Schmidt	21-5	10-4	1961	Glen Rose	14-10	5-9
1925	Francis Schmidt	23-2	11-1	1962	Glen Rose	13-11	8-6
1926	Francis Schmidt	14-2	8-2	1963	Glen Rose	9-14	6-8
1927	Francis Schmidt	19-1	12-0	1964	Glen Rose	9-14	5-9
1928	Francis Schmidt	19-1	11-1	1965	Glen Rose	13-10	7-7
1929	Charles Bassett	16-7	10-2	1966	Duddy Waller	6-17	4-10
1930	Charles Bassett	14-9	7-5	1967	Duddy Waller	10-14	7-7
1931	Charles Bassett	18-6	8-4	1968	Duddy Waller	10-14	4-10
1932	Charles Bassett	14-7	6-6	1969	Duddy Waller	5-19	3-11
1933	Glen Rose	16-8	6-6	1970	Lanny Van Eman	5-21	1-13
1934	Glen Rose	14-5	9-3	1971	Lanny Van Eman	8-18	5-9
1935	Glen Rose	24-3	11-1	1972	Lanny Van Eman	16-10	9-5
1936	Glen Rose	12-6	8-4	1973	Eddie Sutton	10-16	6-8
1937	Glen Rose	19-3	11-1	1974	Eddie Sutton	17-9	11-3
1938	Glen Rose	18-5	9-3	1975	Eddie Sutton	19-9	9-7
1939	Glen Rose	12-10	6-6	1976	Eddie Sutton	26-2	16-0
1940	Glen Rose	20-3	12-0	1977	Eddie Sutton	32-4	14-2
1941	Glen Rose	19-4	10-2	1978	Eddie Sutton	25-5	13-3
1942	Glen Rose	19-7	8-4	1979	Eddie Sutton	21-8	13-3
1943	Eugene Lambert	16-8	11-1	1980	Eddie Sutton	24-8	13-3
1944	Eugene Lambert	17-9	9-3	1981	Eddie Sutton	23-6	12-4
1945	Eugene Lambert	16-7	9-3	1982	Eddie Sutton	26-4	14-2
1946	Eugene Lambert	14-10	8-4	1983	Eddie Sutton	25-7	14-2
1947	Eugene Lambert	16-8	8-4	1984	Eddie Sutton	22-13	10-6
1948	Eugene Lambert	15-11	9-3	1985	Nolan Richardson	12-16	4-12
1949	Presley Askew	12-12	8-4	1986	Nolan Richardson	19-14	8-8
1950	Presley Askew	13-11	7-5	1987	Nolan Richardson	21-9	11-5
1951	Presley Askew	10-14	4-8	1988	Nolan Richardson	25-7	13-3
1952	Glen Rose	10-11	4-8	1989	Nolan Richardson	30-5	14-2
1953	Glen Rose	13-9	6-6	1990	Nolan Richardson	34-4	15-1
1954	Glen Rose	14-9	8-4	1991	Nolan Richardson	26-8	13-3
1955	Glen Rose	11-12	9-3	1992	Nolan Richardson	22-9	10-6
1956	Glen Rose	11-12	5-7	1993	Nolan Richardson	31-3	14-2
1957	Glen Rose	17-10	9-5	1994	Nolan Richardson	32-7	12-4
1958	Glen Rose	9-14	6-8	1995	Nolan Richardson	20-13	9-7
1959	Glen Rose	12-11	7-7				

COACHING RECORDS

Year	Coach	Yrs.	W	L	Pct.
1923-29	Francis Schmidt	6	113	22	.837
1929-33	Charles Bassett	4	62	29	.681
1933-42	Glen Rose	9	154	47	.766
1942-49	Eugene Lambert	7	113	60	.653
1949-52	Presley Askew	3	35	37	.486
1952-66	Glenn Rose	14	171	154	.526
1966-70	Duddy Waller	4	31	64	.326
1970-74	Lanny Van Eman	4	39	65	.375
1974-85	Eddie Sutton	11	260	75	.776
1985-	Nolan Richardson	11	272	95	.746
Totals		73	1250	648	.659

POSTSEASON RESULTS

NCAA PLAYOFFS

(Total Record 37-22)
1996 EAST REGIONAL
    Arkansas 86, Penn State 80
    Arkansas 65, Marquette 56
    Massachusetts 79, Arkansas 63
1995 MIDWEST REGIONAL
    Arkansas 79, Texas Southern 78
    Arkansas 96, Syracuse 94 (OT)
    Arkansas 96, Memphis 91 (OT)
    Arkansas 68, Virginia 61
    FINAL FOUR
    Arkansas 75, North Carolina 68
    UCLA 89, Arkansas 78
1994 MIDWEST REGIONAL
    Arkansas 94, North Carolina A&T 79
    Arkansas 85, Georgetown 73
    Arkansas 103, Tulsa 84 (semifinals)
    Arkansas 76, Michigan 68 (finals)
    FINAL FOUR:
    Arkansas 91, Arizona 82
    Arkansas 76, Duke 72 (championship)
1993 EAST REGIONAL
    Arkansas 94, Holy Cross 64 (1st round)
    Arkansas 80, St. John's 74 (2nd round)
    North Carolina 80, Arkansas 74 (semifinals)
1992 MIDWEST REGIONAL:
    Arkansas 80, Murray State 69 (1st round)
    Memphis State 82, Arkansas 80 (2nd round)
1991 SOUTHEAST REGIONAL
    Arkansas 117, Georgia State 76 (1st round)
    Arkansas 97, Arizona State 90 (2nd round)
    Arkansas 93, Alabama 70 (semifinals)
    Kansas 93, Arkansas 81 (finals)
1990 MIDWEST REGIONAL
    Arkansas 68, Princeton 64 (1 st round)
    Arkansas 86, Dayton 84 (2nd round)
    Arkansas 96, North Carolina 73 (semifinals)
    Arkansas 88, Texas 85 (finals)
1990 FINAL FOUR:
    Duke 97, Arkansas 83
1989 MIDWEST REGIONAL
    Arkansas 120, Loyola-Marymount 101 (1st rnd)
    Louisville 93, Arkansas 74 (2nd round)
1988 SOUTHEAST REGIONAL
    Villanova 82, Arkansas 74 (1st round)
1985 WEST REGIONAL
    Arkansas 63, Iowa 53 (1st round)
    St. John's 68, Arkansas 65 (2nd round)
1984 EAST REGIONAL
    Virginia 53, Arkansas 51 (1st round)
1983 MIDEAST REGIONAL
    Arkansas 78, Purdue 68 (2nd round)
    Louisville 65, Arkansas 63 (semifinals)
1982 MIDWEST REGIONAL
    Kansas State 65, Arkansas 64 (2nd round)
1981 MIDWEST REGIONAL
    Arkansas 73, Mercer 67 (1st round)
    Arkansas 74, Louisville 73 (2nd round)
    LSU 72, Arkansas 56 (semifinals)
1980 MIDWEST REGIONAL
    Kansas State 71, Arkansas 53 (1st round)
1979 MIDWEST REGIONAL
    Arkansas 74, Weber State 63 (1st round)
    Arkansas 73, Louisville 62 (semifinals)
    Indiana State 73, Arkansas 71 (championship)
1978 FAR WEST REGIONAL
    Arkansas 73, Weber State 52 (2nd round)

    Arkansas 74, UCLA 70 (semifinals)
    Arkansas 61, Cal-State Fullerton 58
      (championship)
1978 FINAL FOUR
    Kentucky 64, Arkansas 59 (semifinals)
    Arkansas 71, Notre Dame 69 (third place game)
1977 MIDWEST REGIONAL
    Wake Forest 86, Arkansas 80 (1st round)
1958 WESTERN REGIONAL
    Oklahoma State 65, Arkansas 40 (1st round)
    Cincinnati 97, Arkansas 62 (consolation)
1949 WESTERN REGIONAL
    Oregon State 56, Arkansas 38 (1st round)
    Arkansas 64, Wyoming 40 (3rd place)
1945 WESTERN PLAYOFF
    Arkansas 79, Oregon 76 (1st round)
    FINAL FOUR:
    Oklahoma A&M 68, Arkansas 41 (semifinals)
1944 SWC
    champion Arkansas prevented from playing
    due to automobile accident to several players
1941 WESTERN PLAYOFF
    Arkansas 52, Wyoming 40 (1st round)
1941 FINAL FOUR
    Washington State 64, Arkansas 53 (semifinals)

SEC POSTSEASON TOURNAMENT

(Total Record: 6-5)
1992: Arkansas 73, Georgia 60
    Alabama 90, Arkansas 89 (semifinals)
1993: Arkansas 65, Georgia 60
    Kentucky 92, Arkansas 82 (semifinals)
1994: Arkansas 95, Georgia 83
    Kentucky 90, Arkansas 78 (semifinals)
1995: Arkansas 73, Vanderbilt 72
    Arkansas 69, Alabama 58
    Kentucky 95, Arkansas 94 (OT) (finals)
1996: Arkansas 80, South Carolina 58
    Kentucky 95, Arkansas 75

NIT TOURNAMENT

(Total Record: 4-2)
1987 Arkansas 67, Arkansas State 64 (OT)
    Nebraska 78, Arkansas 71 (2nd round)
1990 (Pre-Season):
    Arkansas 107, Vanderbilt 70
    Arkansas 98, Duke 88
    Arkansas 110, Oklahoma 88
    Arizona 89, Arkansas 77

TEAM RECORDS

POINTS

Game: 166 vs. U.S. International,12/9/89 at Fayetteville
Season: 3,783, 1991
SEC Game: 117 vs. Auburn, 1/15/94
SEC Season: 1,468,1992

FIELD GOALS

Game: 68 vs. U.S. International,12/9/89
Season: 1,414, 1991
SEC Game: 43 vs. Auburn, 1/15/94
SEC Season: 529, 1992

FIELD GOALS ATTEMPTED

Game: 101 vs. U.S. International, 12/9/89
Season: 2,820 1991
SEC Game: 88 vs. Mississippi State, 2/20/93
SEC Season: 1,075, 1992

FIELD GOAL PERCENTAGE

Game: .794 vs. Texas Tech, 2/20/79 (27 of 34)
Season: .546,1978 (1,060)
SEC Game: .621 vs. Mississippi State, 2/20/93
SEC Season: .497, 1993 (521 of 1049)

FREE THROWS

Game: 46, vs. TCU, 3/1/55
Season: 713, 1991
SEC Game: 41 vs. Kentucky,1/25/92
SEC Season: 300, 1992

FREE THROWS ATTEMPTED

Game: 65, vs. TCU, 3/1/55
Season: 975, 1991
SEC Game: 49 vs. Kentucky 1/25/92
SEC Season: 815,1992

FREE THROW PERCENTAGE

Game: 1.000, vs. Texas Tech,1/8/66 (12 of 12)
Season: .777,1962 (502 of 646)
SEC Game: .857, vs. Alabama,1/8/92 (6 of 7)
SEC Season: 750 (300 of 400)

THREE POINT FIELD GOALS

Game: 20 vs. Texas Southern, 12/28/93
Season: 361, 1995
SEC Game: 17 vs. Auburn, 1/15/95
SEC Season: 143, 1995

THREE POINT FIELD GOALS ATTEMPTED

Game: 45 vs. Delaware State, 12/11/93
Season: 917, 1995
SEC Game: 36 vs. Auburn, 1/15/95
SEC Season: 364, 1995

THREE POINT FIELD GOAL PERCENTAGE

Game: .833, (5-6) vs. Delaware State,12/26/89
Season: .395 (210-532), 1992-1993
SEC Game: .625 (10-16) vs. Auburn, 1/4/92
SEC Season: .400 (110-275),1992

REBOUNDS

Game: 75 vs. Fort Chaffee,12/22/56
Season: 1,540,1991
SEC Game: 61 vs. Ole Miss,1/18/92
SEC Season: 616, 1994

SCORING AVERAGE

Season: 99.6, 1991
SEC Season: 91.8,1992
Rebound Average
Season: 52.0, 1974
SEC Season: 37.0, 1995

CONSECUTIVE WINNING SEASONS

26 (1923-24; 1948-49)

CONSECUTIVE NON-LOSING SEASONS

27 (1923-24, 1949-50)

CONSECUTIVE SEASON OPENING WINS

25 (1923-24; 1947-48)

LONGEST WINNING STREAK

31 Games (1927-29)

CONSECUTIVE CONFERENCE WINS

21 (1926-29)

CONSECUTIVE CONFERENCE LOSSES

9 (1970-71)

MOST GAMES

39 (94-95)

MOST WINS

34 (90-91)

MOST LOSSES

21 (70-71)

FEWEST WINS

5 (69-70, 70-71)

FEWEST LOSSES

1 (27-28, 28-29)

FEWEST POINTS

519 (16 games 1926-27)
643 (20 games or more 1929-30)

GREATEST SCORING MARGIN

19.2 (90-91)

LOWEST SCORING AVERAGE

28.0 (29-30, 643 in 23 games)

BEST WINNING PERCENTAGE

.950 (19 wins 1 loss; 1927-28, 1928-29)

WORST WINNING PERCENTAGE

.192 (5 wins 21 losses, 1970-71)

MOST POINTS ALLOWED

3115 (1994-95; 39 games)

FEWEST POINTS ALLOWED

374 (16 games; 1926-27)
448 (20 games or more 1925-26)

LONGEST LOSING STREAK

10 games (1970-71)

FEWEST PERSONAL FOULS

434 (1965-66)

MOST REBOUNDS

1540 (1990-91)

FEWEST REBOUNDS

862 (1981-82)

BIGGEST VICTORY MARGIN

82 vs. Bethune-Cookman (Arkansas 128, Bethune-Cookman 46, Dec. 4, 1991)

SMALLEST VICTORY MARGIN

56 one-point games (Last game 79-78 vs. Texas Southern, 3-17-94)

BIGGEST DEFEAT MARGIN

51 vs. Ole Miss (Ole Miss 117, Arkansas 66, 12-10-73)

SMALLEST DEFEAT MARGIN

56 one-point games (Last game 71-72 vs. Mississippi State, 1-19-94)

MOST POINTS IN A LOSING GAME

110 vs. Baylor 111 OT, 3-2-71

ALL-TIME OVERTIME RECORD

29-19 (5-2 in 2 OT; 0-1 in 3OT)

LAST OVERTIME GAME

3-17-95; Arkansas 96, Memphis 91

LAST TWO-OVERTIME GAME

2-24-87; Arkansas 100, Texas A&M 97

LAST THREE-OVERTIME GAME

2-9-80; Houston 90, Arkansas 84

MOST OVERTIME GAMES, SEASON

5 in 1985-86 (3 wins, 2 losses)

MOST POINTS HOME FLOOR, GAME

166 vs. US International 101, 12-9-89

MOST POINTS OPPONENT FLOOR, GAME

117 (Arkansas 117, Auburn 105, 1-15-94)

MOST POINTS NEUTRAL FLOOR, GAME

120 (Arkansas 120, Texas 89, 3-10-91; Arkansas 120, Loyola-Marymount 101, 3-16-89)

MOST POINTS FIRST HALF, GAME

78 vs. US International,12-9-89

MOST POINTS SECOND HALF, GAME

88 vs. US International, 12-9-89

MOST POINTS IN OVERTIME, GAME

19 vs. LSU, 3-3-92; Arkansas 106, LSU 92

FEWEST COMBINED POINTS, GAME

28 (SMU 17, Arkansas 11 in 1923)

FEWEST POINTS ALLOWED, GAME

6 (Arkansas 64, Fort Smith National Guard 6 in 1925) Modern Record since 1935- 14 (Arkansas 39, Baylor 14 in 1936)

ASSISTS, GAME

47 vs. US International, 12-9-89

BLOCKS, GAME

16 vs. Texas, 2-4-90

STEALS, GAME

21 vs. Mississippi State, 1-15-92

FEWEST TURNOVERS, GAME

4 vs. Texas, 2-2-80

FIELD GOALS MADE, GAME

1. 68 vs. U.S. International, 1990
2. 51 vs. Baylor, 1972
3. 50 vs. Montevallo, 1994
   50 vs. Quincy College, 1992
5. 48 vs. Montevallo, 1995
   48 vs. Delaware State, 1994
   48 vs. Bethune-Cookman, 1992
   48 vs. TCU, 1976
   48 vs. Jackson State, 1992
10. 47, vs. Centenary, 1995
    47 vs. Oklahoma, 1991
    47 vs. Loyola-Marymount, 1989
    47 vs. Oklahoma, 1991
14. 46 vs. Texas Southern, 1994
    46 vs. Rice, 1974

FIELD GOALS ATTEMPTED, GAME

1. 101 vs. U.S. Int'l., 1990
2. 97 vs. Western Kentucky,1974
3. 95 vs. Texas, 1957
4. 94 vs. Jackson State, 1991
   94 vs. TCU, 1964
   94 vs. Jackson State, 1992

FIELD GOAL PERCENTAGE, GAME

1. .794 vs. Texas Tech, 1979 (27 of 34)
2. .744 vs. Baylor, 1979 (29 of 39)
3. .727 vs. Alabama State, 1984 (32 of 44)
4. .707 vs. Rice, 1978 (29 of 41)
5. .683 vs. SMU, 1984 (28 of 41)
6. .680 vs. Wake Forest, 197 (34 of 50)
7. .679 vs. Rice, 1983 (36 of 53)
8. .676 vs. Texas, 1985 (25 of 37)
9. .673 vs. U.S. International, 1990 (68 of 101)
   .673 vs. SE Missouri State, 1984 (37 of 55)
11. .671 vs. Baylor, 1990
12. .667 vs. Texas A&M, 1982 (34 of 51)
    .667 vs. Nebraska, 198 (26 of 39)
    .667 vs. TCU, 1978 (28 of 42)
    .667 vs. SW Missouri State, 1979 (38 of 57)

FREE THROWS MADE, GAME

1. 46 vs. TCU, 1955
2. 41 vs. Kentucky, 1992
   41 vs. Rice, 1972

FREE THROWS ATTEMPTED, GAME

1. 65 vs. TCU, 1955
2. 55 vs. Rice, 1972
3. 49 vs. Kentucky, 1992
   49 vs. NE Louisiana, 1991
   48 vs. SMU, 1972
   48 vs. Baylor, 1956
7. 47 vs. Centenary, 1968
8. 45 vs. Fort Chaffee, 1957
   45 vs. Ole Miss, 1995
10. 44 vs. Kansas, 1987
    44 vs. San Francisco State, 1972

REBOUNDS, GAME

1. 75 vs. Fort Chaffee, 1957
2. 73 vs. Rice, 1960
3. 72 vs. Texas, 1957
4. 71 vs. Rockhurst, 1972
5. 71 vs. Ole Miss, 1965

FREE THROW PERCENTAGE, GAME

1. 1.000 vs. Centenary, 1975 (12 of 12)
   1.000 vs. Texas Tech, 1966 (12 of 12)
3. .952 vs. SMU, 1978 (20 of 21)
4. .941 vs. Houston, 1978 (16 of 17)
5. .938 vs. Rice, 1982 (30 of 32)
6. .937 vs. TCU, 1959 (15 of 16)
7. .923 vs. SMU, 1978 (12 of 13)
   .923 vs. SMU, 1961 (12 of 13)
   .923 vs. Tennessee, 1993 (12 of 13)
10. .917 vs. South Carolina, 1994 (11 of 12)
    .917 vs. Texas, 1966 (22 of 24)
    .917 vs. Texas Tech, 1963 (33 of 36)

INDIVIDUAL RECORDS

POINTS

Game: 47, Martin Terry vs. SMU, 2/24/73
Season: 786, Todd Day, 1991
Career: 2,395, Todd Day, 1988-92

SCORING AVERAGE

Season: 28.3, Martin Terry, 1973 (735 in 26 games)
Career: 26.3, Martin Terry, 1971-73

FIELD GOALS

Game: 20, Dean Tolson vs. Texas A&M, 3/2/74
Season: 294, Joe Kleine, 1985
Career: 835, Todd Day, 1988-92

FIELD GOALS ATTEMPTED

Game: 36, Dean Tolson vs. Texas A&M, 3/2/74
Season: 586, Todd Day, 1991
Career: 1,744, Todd Day, 1988-92

FIELD GOAL PERCENTAGE

(8 shot min.)
Game: 1.000, Isaiah Morris (8-8) vs. Miss. St.,
   1/15/92; Daryll Saulsberry (10-10) vs.
   MacMurray,1/4/75; Steve Schall (9-9) vs. Weber
   State, 3/11/79; Joe Kleine (8-8) vs. St. Peter's,
   12/28/83
Season: .704, Oliver Miller (254-361), 1991
Career: .636, Oliver Miller (680-1069), 1988-92

FREE THROWS

Game: 22, Martin Terry vs. Texas A&M, 1/22/72
Season: 212, Sidney Moncrief, 1979
Career: 588, Sidney Moncrief, 1975-79

FREE THROWS ATTEMPTED

Game: 24, Martin Terry vs. Texas A&M, 1/22/72
Season: 304, Corliss Williamson, 1995
Career: 752, Sidney Moncrief, 1975-79

FREE THROW PERCENTAGE

(Min. 12 attempts)
Game: 1000 Tommy Boyer (18-18) vs. Texas Tech,
   2/19/63; Scott Hastings (14-14) vs. Rice, 2/20/82;
   Ron Huery (12-12) vs. California, 2/30/86
Season: .939, Rickey Medlock (62 of 66), 1975
Career: .904, Rickey Medlock (178 of 197), 1973-75

THREE POINT FIELD GOALS

Game: 12, Al Dillard vs. Delaware State, 12-11-93
Season: 102, Scotty Thurman, 1995
Career: 267, Scotty Thurman, 1993-95

THREE POINT FIELD GOALS ATTEMPTED

Game: 22, Al Dillard vs. Delaware State, 12-11-93
Season: 239, Scotty Thurman, 1995
Career: 618, Scotty Thurman, 1993-95

THREE POINT FIELD GOAL PERCENTAGE

(4 shots per game)
Game: 1.000 Dwight Stewart (4-4) vs. Georgetown,
   3-20-94; Arlyn Bowers (4-4) vs. SMU, 11/14/89;
   Lee Mayberry (4-4) vs. Rice, 3/1/89
Season: .504, Lee Mayberry, 1990
Career: .432, Scotty Thurman, 1993-95

REBOUNDS

Game: 22, Dean Tolson vs. Rice, 3/3/73; Dean Tolson
   vs. Texas, 1/20/73 22; Dean Tolson vs. TCU,
   2/12/72
Season: 310, Dean Tolson, 1973
Career: 1,015, Sidney Moncrief, 1975-79

REBOUNDING AVERAGE

Season: 12.4, Dean Tolson, 1973 (310 in 25 games)
Career: 11.0, Dean Tolson, 1972-74

ASSISTS

Game: 14, Kareem Reid vs. LSU, 3/2/96
Season: 219, Kareem Reid, 1995-96
Career: 729, Lee Mayberry, 1988-92

STEALS

Game: 9, Robert Shepherd vs. Arizona, 12/6/93
Season: 102, Clint McDaniel, 1995
Career: 291, Lee Mayberry, 1988-92

BLOCKED SHOTS

Game: 10, Oliver Miller vs. Texas, 2/4/90
Season: 112, Oliver Miller, 1991
Career: 345, Oliver Miller, 1988-92

PERSONAL FOULS

Season: 132, Corey Beck, 1995
Career: 413, Oliver Miller, 1989-92

TOTAL POINTS, GAME

1. 47, Martin Terry vs. SMU, 1973
2. 46, Martin Terry vs. Texas A&M, 1972
3. 45, Dean Tolson vs. Texas A&M, 1974
4. 43, Todd Day vs. LSU, 1992
   43, Martin Terry vs. Memphis State, 1973

FIELD GOALS MADE, GAME

1. 20, Dean Tolson vs. Texas A&M, 1974
2. 17, Martin Terry vs. Southern Illinois, 1972
3. 16, Todd Day vs. LSU, 1992
   16, Dean Tolson vs. Indiana State, 1974
   16, Martin Terry vs. SMU, 1973
   16, Vernon Murphy vs. Missouri-St. Louis, 1971

FIELD GOALS ATTEMPTED, GAME

1. 30, Dean Tolson vs. TCU, 1972
2. 29, Martin Terry vs. SMU, 1973
   29, Terry Day vs. Oklahoma, 1957
4. 28, Ronnie Garner vs. SMU, 1960
5. 27, Martin Terry vs. TCU, 1973

FREE THROWS MADE, GAME

1. 22, Martin Terry vs. Texas A&M, 1972
2. 19, Vernon Murphy vs. Missouri-St. Louis, 1971
3. 18, Tommy Boyer vs. Texas Tech, 1963
4. 17, Corliss Williamson vs. Ole Miss, 1995
   17, Martin Terry vs. Tulane, 1973

FREE THROWS ATTEMPTED, GAME

1. 24, Martin Terry vs. Texas A&M, 1972
2. 23, Vernon Murphy vs. Oklahoma, 1971
3. 22, Corliss Williamson vs. Ole Miss, 1995
   22, Lawrence Stolzer vs. Ft. Chaffee, 1957
5. 21, Martin Terry vs. Tulane, 1973

TOTAL POINTS, SEASON

1. 786, Todd Day, 1991
2. 773, Joe Kleine, 1985
3. 770, Corliss Williamson, 1995
4. 735, Martin Terry, 1973
5. 695, Corliss Williamson, 1994
6. 684, Todd Day, 1990
7. 660, Sidney Moncrief, 1979
8. 647, Ron Brewer, 1978
9. 633, Martin Terry, 1972
10. 621, Sidney Moncrief, 1978
11. 596, Oliver Miller, 1991
12. 588, Marvin Delph, 1978
13. 581, Joe Kleine, 1984
14. 571, Scotty Thurman, 1995
15. 552, Marvin Delph, 1977

FIELD GOALS MADE, SEASON

1. 294, Joe Kleine, 1985
2. 283, Corliss Williamson, 1995
3. 277, Todd Day, 1991
4. 273, Corliss Williamson, 1994
5. 264, Martin Terry, 1973
6. 258, Ron Brewer, 1978
7. 254, Oliver Miller, 1991
8. 253, Marvin Delph, 1978
9. 245, Marvin Delph, 1977
10. 237, Todd Day, 1990
11. 224, Sidney Moncrief, 1979
12. 213, Martin Terry, 1972
13. 209, Joe Kleine, 1984
    209, Sidney Moncrief, 1978
15. 206, Scotty Thurman, 1995

FIELD GOALS ATTEMPTED, SEASON

1. 586, Todd Day, 1991
2. 515, Corliss Williamson, 1995
3. 508, Martin Terry, 1973
4. 486, Ron Brewer, 1978
5. 484, Joe Kleine, 1985

FREE THROWS MADE, SEASON

1. 212, Sidney Moncrief, 1979
2. 207, Martin Terry, 1973
   207, Martin Terry, 1972
4. 203, Corliss Williamson, 1995
   203, Sidney Moncrief, 1978
6. 185, Joe Kleine, 1985
7. 165, Todd Day, 1991
8. 163, Joe Kleine, 1984
9. 152, Darrell Walker, 1983
10. 149, Corliss Williamson, 1994

FREE THROWS ATTEMPTED, SEASON

1. 304, Corliss Williamson, 1995
2. 261, Martin Terry, 1972
3. 257, Joe Kleine, 1985
4. 256, Sidney Moncrief, 1978
5. 248, Sidney Moncrief, 1979

REBOUNDS, SEASON

1. 310, Dean Tolson, 1973
2. 294, Oliver Miller, 1991
   294, Joe Kleine, 1985
4. 293, Corliss Williamson, 1995
   293, Joe Kleine, 1984
6. 289, Sidney Moncrief, 1979
7. 278, Sidney Moncrief, 1978
   278, Dean Tolson, 1974
9. 262, Corliss Williamson, 1994
10. 261, Oliver Miller, 1992
11. 257, Dean Tolson, 1972
12. 240, Andrew Lang, 1987
13. 235, Sidney Moncrief, 1977
14. 233, Ronnie Garner, 1960
    233, Manual Whitley, 1956

REBOUND AVERAGE, SEASON

1. 12.4, Dean Tolson, 1973 (310 in 25 games)
2. 10.7, Dean Tolson, 1974 (278 in 26 games)
3. 9.9, Dean Tolson, 1972 (257 in 26 games)
4. 9.7, Ronnie Garner, 1960 (233 in 24 games)
5. 9.7, Manuel Whitley, 1956 (233 in 24 games)

STEALS, SEASON

1. 102, Clint McDaniel, 1995
2. 100, Lee Mayberry, 1990-91
3. 97, Keith Wilson, 1988-89
4. 92, Alvin Robertson, 1983-84
5. 88, Alvin Robertson, 1982-83

ASSISTS, SEASON

1. 219, Kareem Reid, 1995-96
2. 209, Lee Mayberry, 1990-91
3. 207, Corey Beck, 1995
4. 202, Lee Mayberry, 1991-92
5. 191, Alvin Robertson, 1983-84
6. 183, Lee Mayberry, 1989-90
7. 169, Corey Beck, 1994
8. 143, William Mills, 1984-85
9. 138, Keith Wilson, 1988-89
10. 135, Lee Mayberry, 1988-89

CAREER BESTS

TOTAL POINTS

1. 2,395, Todd Day, 1988-92
2. 2,066, Sidney Moncrief, 1975-79
3. 1,940, Lee Mayberry, 1988-92
4. 1,779, Scott Hastings,1978-82
5. 1,753, Joe Kleine,1982-85
6. 1,742, Marvin Delph, 1974-78
7. 1,728, Corliss Williamson, 1993-95
8. 1,674, Oliver Miller,1988-92
9. 1,650, Scotty Thurman, 1993-95
10. 1,644, George Kok,1945-49
11. 1,550, Ron Huery,1986-91
12. 1,440, Ron Brewer, 1975-78
13. 1,368, Martin Terry,1972-73
14. 1,325, Darrell Walker,1980-83
15. 1,316, Dean Tolson,1972-74

SCORING AVERAGE

1. 26.3, Martin Terry 1972-73 (1,368 pts. in 52 games)
2. 18.9, Todd Day 1988-92 (2,395 pts. in 127 games)
3. 18.3, Dean Tolson 1972-74 (1,316 pts. in 72 games)
4. 18.1, Joe Kleine 1982-85 (1,753 pts. in 97 games)
5. 17.3, Almer Lee 1970-72 (897 pts. in 52 games)

FIELD GOALS MADE

1. 835 Todd Day,1988-92
2. 762, Marvin Delph, 1974-78
3. 739, Sidney Moncrief, 1975-79
4. 723, Lee Mayberry, 1988-91
5. 680, Oliver Miller, 1988-91
6. 668, Joe Kleine, 1982-85
7. 665, Scott Hastings, 1978-82
8. 657, Corliss Williamson, 1993-95
9. 611, Scotty Thurman, 1993-95
10. 587, Ron Brewer, 1975-78
11. 551, Dean Tolson,1972-74
12. 534, Ron Huery,1986-91
13. 496, Darrell Walker, 1980-83
14. 477, Martin Terry,1972-73
15. 445, James Eldridge,1968-70

FIELD GOALS ATTEMPTED

1. 1,744, Todd Day,1988-92
2. 1,460, Lee Mayberry, 1988-92
3. 1,440, Marvin Delph, 1974-78
4. 1,318, Scotty Thurman, 1993-95
5. 1,223, Scott Hastings, 1978-82
6. 1,220, Sidney Moncrief, 1975-79
7. 1,156, Ron Huery, 1986-91
8. 1,142, Joe Kleine, 1982-85
9. 1,127, Corliss Williamson, 1993-95
10. 1,069, Oliver Miller, 1988-92
    1,069, Dean Tolson,1972-74
12. 1,038, Ron Brewer, 1975-78
13. 962, Martin Terry, 1972-73
14. 959, Darrell Walker, 1980-83
15. 952, James Eldridge, 1968-70

FREE THROWS MADE

1. 588, Sidney Moncrief, 1975-79
2. 499, Todd Day, 1988-92
3. 449, Scott Hastings, 1978-82
4. 417, Joe Kleine, 1982-85
5. 414, Martin Terry, 1972-73
6. 413, Corliss Williamson, 1993-95
7. 388, Ron Huery, 1986-91
8. 333, Darrell Walker, 1980-83
9. 315, Tommy Boyer, 1961-63
10. 309, Oliver Miller, 1988-92
11. 308, U.S. Reed, 1977-81

12. 300, Jerry Carlton, 1960-62
13. 280, Corey Beck, 1993-95
14. 276, Lee Mayberry, 1988-92
15. 273, Pat Foster, 1959-61

FREE THROWS ATTEMPTED

1. 752, Sidney Moncrief,1975-79
2. 668, Todd Day, 1988-92
3. 615, Corliss Williamson, 1993-95
4. 600, Scott Hastings, 1978-82
5. 577, Joe Kleine, 1982-85
6. 524, Darrell Walker, 1980-83
7. 503, Martin Terry, 1972-73
8. 494, Ron Huery, 1986-91
9. 478, Oliver Miller, 1988-92
10. 419, U.S. Reed, 1977-81
11. 418, Corey Beck, 1993-95
12. 412, Dean Tolson, 1972-74
13. 401, Clyde Rhoden, 1959-61
14. 381, Lee Mayberry, 1988-92
15. 361, Robert McKenzie, 1968-70

REBOUNDS

1. 1,015, Sidney Moncrief,1975-79
2. 886 Oliver Miller, 1988-92
3. 845 Dean Tolson, 1972-74
4. 806, Joe Kleine, 1982-85
5. 693, Andrew Lang,1985-88
6. 680, Scott Hastings,1978-82
7. 673, Todd Day, 1988-92
8. 647, Corliss Williamson, 1993-95
9. 609, Marvin Delph,1974-78
10. 516, James Eldridge,1968-70
11. 488, Terry Day,1955-57
12. 484, Dennis White, 1972-74
13. 472, J.D. McConnell,1964-66
14. 464, Clyde Rhoden,1959-61
15. 463, Darrell Walker,1980-83

REBOUND AVERAGE

1. 11.0, Dean Tolson 1972-74 (845 in 77 games)
2. 8.3, Sidney Moncrief 1975-79 (1,015 in 122 games)
   8.3, Vernon Murphy 1970-71 (282 in 34 games)
4. 8.2, Kent Allison 1975 (213 in 26 games)
5. 7.7, Manuel Whitely 1953-56 (374 in 45 games)

ASSISTS

1. 729, Lee Mayberry, 1988-92
2. 351, Ron Huery, 1986-91
3. 341, Alvin Robertson, 1981-84
4. 319, Todd Day, 1988-92
5. 303, Keith Wilson, 1986-89
6. 302, Darrell Walker, 1980-83
7. 296, Oliver Miller, 1988-92
8. 276, Corey Beck, 1993-94
9. 243, Arlyn Bowers, 1988-91
   243, Allie Freeman, 1984-88

STEALS

1. 291, Lee Mayberry, 1988-92
2. 271, Todd Day, 1988-92
3. 230, Darrell Walker, 1980-83
4. 217, Alvin Robertson, 1981-84
5. 207, Ron Huery, 1986-91
6. 188, Keith Wilson, 1986-89
7. 171, Ron Brewer, 1975-78
8. 152, Sidney Moncrief, 1975-79
9. 144, Robert Shepherd, 1991-93
10. 119, Arlyn Bowers, 1988-91
    119, U.S. Reed, 1977-81

YEARLY LEADERS

SCORING

Year	Name	Games	Points	Avg.
1995-96	Kareem Reid	33	426	12.9
1994-95	Corliss Williamson	39	770	19.7
1993-94	Corliss Williamson	34	695	20.4
1992-93	Scotty Thurman	31	540	17.4
1991-92	Lee Mayberry	34	500	15.2
1990-91	Todd Day	38	786	20.7
1989-90	Todd Day	35	684	19.5
1988-89	Lenzie Howell	32	466	14.6
1987-88	Ron Huery	30	403	13.4
1986-87	Tim Scott	33	393	11.9
1985-86	Mike Ratliff	28	368	13.1
1984-85	Joe Kleine	35	773	22.1
1983-84	Joe Kleine	32	581	18.2
1982-83	Darrell Walker	30	546	18.2
1981-82	Scott Hastings	29	539	18.6
1980-81	Scott Hastings	32	523	16.3
1979-80	Scott Hastings	29	469	16.2
1978-79	Sidney Moncrief	30	660	22.0
1977-78	Ron Brewer	36	647	18.0
1976-77	Marvin Delph	28	552	19.7
1975-76	Marvin Delph	27	440	16.3
1974-75	Kent Allison	26	393	15.1
1973-74	Dean Tolson	26	472	22.5
1972-73	Martin Terry	26	735	28.3
1971-72	Martin Terry	26	633	24.3
1970-71	Almer Lee	23	441	19.2
1969-70	Almer Lee	24	409	17.0
1968-69	James Eldridge	24	328	13.7
1967-68	James Eldridge	24	398	16.6
1966-67	Tommy Rowland	24	443	18.5
1965-66	Ricky Sugg	24	328	13.6
1964-65	Ricky Sugg	24	340	14.2
1963-64	Jim Magness	24	356	14.8
1962-63	Tommy Boyer	24	439	18.3
1961-62	Jerry Carlton	24	438	18.2
1960-61	Pat Foster	23	355	15.4
1959-60	Clyde Rhoden	24	389	16.2
1958-59	Clyde Rhoden	24	350	14.6
1957-58	Fred Grim	27	380	14.1
1956-57	Terry Day	24	301	12.5
1955-56	Manuel Whitely	24	407	17.0
1954-55	Jerald Barnett	24	247	10.3
1953-54	Jerald Barnett	23	225	9.8
1952-53	Gene Lambert, Jr.	21	270	12.9
1951-52	Walter Kearns	24	216	9.0
1950-51	Billy Hester	22	201	9.1
1949-50	Jim Cathcart	23	233	10.1
1948-49	Bob Ambler	26	259	10.0
1947-48	George Kok	23	469	20.4
1946-47	Al Williams	24	380	15.8

REBOUNDING

Year	Name	Games	Reb.	Avg.
1995-96	Derek Hood	33	200	6.1
1994-95	Corliss Williamson	39	293	7.5
1993-94	Corliss Williamson	34	262	7.7
1992-93	Darrell Hawkins	31	140	4.5
1991-92	Oliver Miller	34	261	7.7
1990-91	Oliver Miller	38	294	7.7
1989-90	Oliver Miller	35	219	6.3
1988-89	Lenzie Howell	32	224	7.0
1987-88	Andrew Lang	30	218	7.3
1986-87	Andrew Lang	32	240	7.5
1985-86	Andrew Lang	26	168	6.5
1984-85	Joe Kleine	35	294	8.4
1983-84	Joe Kleine	32	293	9.2
1982-83	Joe Kleine	30	219	7.3
1981-82	Scott Hastings	29	175	6.0
1980-81	Scott Hastings	32	173	5.4
1979-80	Scott Hastings	29	194	6.7
1978-79	Sidney Moncrief	30	289	9.6
1977-78	Sidney Moncrief	36	278	7.7
1976-77	Sidney Moncrief	28	235	8.4
1975-76	Sidney Moncrief	28	213	7.6
1974-75	Kent Allison	26	213	8.2
1973-74	Dean Tolson	26	278	10.6
1972-73	Dean Tolson	25	310	12.4
1971-72	Dean Tolson	26	257	9.9
1970-71	Vernon Murphy	26	230	8.8
1969-70	Robert McKenzie	24	181	7.5
1968-69	James Eldridge	24	169	7.0
1967-68	Gary Stephens	24	182	7.6
1966-67	Tommy Rowland	23	206	9.0
1965-66	John Talkington	23	196	8.5
	J. D. McConnell	23	196	8.5
1964-65	J. D. McConnell	22	153	7.0
1963-64	Jim Magness	23	129	5.6
1962-63	Jim Wilson	24	181	7.5
1961-62	Jim Wilson	24	158	6.6
1960-61	Ronnie Garner	23	180	7.8
1959-60	Ronnie Garner	24	230	9.6
1958-59	Jay Carpenter	24	211	8.8
1957-58	Harry Thompson	24	204	8.5
1956-57	Terry Day	24	216	9.0
1955-56	Manuel Whitely	24	233	9.7
1954-55	Pete Butler	24	173	7.2

HOME RECORDS

Individual: 47, Martin Terry vs. SMU, 2/24/73
Team: 166 vs. U.S. International, 12/9/89
Combined Teams: 267, (UA 166, U.S. Int'l 101), 12/9/89

Individual: 20, Dean Tolson vs. Texas A&M, 3/2/74
Team: 68 vs. U.S. International, 12/9/89

Individiual: 36, Dean Tolson vs. Texas A&M, 3/2/74
Team: 101 vs. U.S. International, 12/9/89
Combined Teams: 201, (UA 97, W. Kentucky, 104), 12/3/74

Individual: 22, Martin Terry vs. Texas A&M, 1/22/72
Team: 41, vs. Rice, 2/5/72
Combined Teams: 72, (UA 41, Rice 31), 2/5/72

Individual: 24, Martin Terry vs. Texas A&M, 1/22/72
Team: 55, vs. Rice, 2/5/72
Combined Teams: 96, (UA 55, Rice 41), 2/5/72

Individual: 22, Dean Tolson vs. TCU, 2/12/72
Team: 75 vs. Fort Chaffee, 12/22/56
Combined Teams: 114, (UA 50, W. Kentucky 64), 2/3/74

FINAL FOUR BOX SCORES

Arkansas 91, Arizona 82
April 2, 1994, Charlotte, North Carolina

Arkansas	FG	3PT	FT	RB	PF	TP
Stewart	2-5	2-3	1-2	5	5	7
Williamson	11-18	0-0	7-9	13	0	29
Robinson	5-9	0-1	2-3	1	2	12
Beck	2-5	1-1	4-8	4	4	9
Thurman	5-13	0-5	4-6	8	2	14
McDaniel	4-10	2-6	2-2	5	3	12
Dillard	2-7	2-7	0-0	1	0	6
Wilson	1-2	0-0	0-2	4	0	2
Rimac	0-1	0-1	0-0	1	0	0
Team Rebounds	4					
Totals	**32-70**	**7-24**	**20-32**	**46**	**16**	**91**

Arizona	FG	3PT	FT	RB	PF	TP
Owes	7-15	0-1	2-2	12	4	16
Geary	2-6	0-3	0-0	4	4	4
Blair	4-7	0-0	0-1	14	3	8
Reeves	6-19	0-9	8-9	4	4	20
Stoudamire	5-24	2-13	4-4	8	4	16
Flanagan	1-1	0-0	0-0	0	1	2
McLean	1-1	0-0	0-0	0	2	2
Williams	5-7	4-6	0-0	6	0	14
Rigdon	0-0	0-0	0-0	0	0	0
Richey	0-0	0-0	0-0	0	0	0
Brown	0-0	0-0	0-0	0	0	0
Kelley	0-0	0-0	0-0	0	0	0
Team Rebounds	2					
Totals	**31-80**	**6-32**	**14-16**	**50**	**23**	**82**

Score by Periods:	1st	2nd	Final
Arkansas	41	50	91
Arizona	41	41	82

Attendance — 23,674

Arkansas 76, Duke 72
April 4, 1994, Charlotte, North Carolina

Arkansas	FG	3PT	FT	RB	PF	TP
Biley	0-0	0-0	0-0	0	1	0
Williamson	10-24	0-0	3-5	8	3	23
Stewart	3-11	0-5	0-0	9	3	6
Beck	5-11	0-1	5-8	10	3	15
Thurman	6-13	3-5	0-0	5	2	15
McDaniel	2-5	1-3	2-4	2	2	7
Robinson	1-5	0-0	0-0	2	1	2
Dillard	1-5	1-4	1-2	1	1	4
Rimac	0-1	0-0	0-0	0	0	0
Wilson	2-2	0-0	0-0	4	1	4
Team Rebounds	2					
Totals	**30-77**	**5-18**	**11-19**	**44**	**17**	**76**

Duke	FG	3PT	FT	RB	PF	TP
Lang	6-9	0-0	3-3	5	5	15
Hill	4-11	1-4	3-5	14	3	12
Parks	7-10	0-0	0-1	7	3	14
Capel	6-16	2-6	0-0	5	3	14
Collins	4-11	4-8	0-0	0	1	12
Clark	1-6	0-2	1-2	1	2	3
Meek	1-2	0-0	0-0	7	1	2
Team Rebounds	5					
Totals	**29-65**	**7-20**	**7-11**	**44**	**18**	**72**

Score by Periods:	1st	2nd	Final
Arkansas	34	42	76
Duke	33	39	72

Attendance — 23,674

Arkansas 75, North Carolina 68
April 1, 1995, Seattle, Washington

Arkansas	FG	3PT	FT	RB	PF	TP
Thurman	2-10	2-9	0-0	5	3	6
Williamson	10-17	0-0	1-1	10	4	21
Martin	1-1	1-1	0-0	1	0	3
McDaniel	3-7	3-5	4-4	5	3	13
Beck	2-9	1-1	0-0	3	3	5
Dillard	0-5	0-4	0-0	0	0	0
Rimac	2-8	2-6	0-0	1	1	6
Stewart	6-10	3-7	0-2	8	2	15
Wilson	1-3	0-0	2-2	4	1	4
Robinson	1-4	0-1	0-0	4	0	2
Team Rebounds	1					
Totals	**28-74**	**12-34**	**7-9**	**42**	**17**	**75**

North Carolina	FG	3PT	FT	RB	PF	TP
Stackhouse	4-7	3-3	7-10	6	2	18
Calabria	1-10	0-7	0-0	5	1	2
Wallace	4-6	0-0	2-4	10	4	10
D.Williams	7-19	5-12	0-0	6	1	19
McInnis	3-9	2-5	5-6	7	4	13
Sullivan	1-2	0-0	2-4	0	0	4
Zwikker	0-1	0-0	0-0	2	1	0
Landry	1-2	0-1	0-0	1	0	2
S.Williams	0-0	0-0	0-0	1	0	0
Team Rebounds	5					
Totals	**21-56**	**10-28**	**16-24**	**43**	**13**	**68**

Score by Periods:	1st	2nd	Final
Arkansas	34	41	75
North Carolina	38	30	68

Attendance — 38,540

UCLA 89, Arkansas 78
April 3, 1995, Seattle, Washington

Arkansas	FG	3PT	FT	RB	PF	TP
Thurman	2-9	1-7	0-0	3	2	5
Williamson	3-16	0-0	6-10	4	1	12
Martin	1-2	1-2	0-0	3	2	3
McDaniel	5-10	3-7	3-4	3	5	16
Beck	4-6	2-3	1-2	3	3	11
Stewart	5-10	1-5	1-2	5	4	12
Dillard	2-4	2-3	0-0	2	1	6
Rimac	1-1	0-0	0-0	2	0	2
Wilson	3-4	0-0	1-2	0	1	7
Williams	0-0	0-0	0-0	0	0	0
Garrett	0-0	0-0	0-0	0	0	0
Team Rebounds	4					
Totals	**28-65**	**10-28**	**12-20**	**31**	**22**	**78**

UCLA	FG	3PT	FT	RB	PF	TP
C.O'Bannon	4-10	0-0	3-4	9	1	11
E.O'Bannon	10-21	1-4	9-11	17	2	30
Zidek	5-8	0-0	4-7	6	4	14
Edney	0-0	0-0	0-0	0	0	0
Bailey	12-20	1-2	1-2	9	3	26
Dollar	1-4	0-1	4-5	3	4	6
Henderson	1-5	0-0	0-0	2	1	2
Team Rebounds	4					
Totals	**33-68**	**2-7**	**21-29**	**50**	**15**	**89**

Score by Periods:	1st	2nd	Final
Arkansas	39	39	78
UCLA	40	49	89

Attendance — 38,540

CENTURY EFFORTS

Arkansas has scored at least 100 points in a game 104 times, including a school record 20 times in 1990-91. Following are the top 30 scoring efforts in school history.

Opponent	Score	Year
U.S. International	166-101	1990
Montevallo	131-63	1994
Baylor	131-109	1972
Texas Southern	129-63	1994
Bethune-Cookman	128-46	1992
Jackson State	126-88	1991
Delaware State	123-66	1994
Quincy College	123-60	1992
Jackson State	123-76	1992
Montevallo	122-64	1995
Centenary	121-94	1994
Missouri	120-68	1994
Texas	120-89	1991
Loyola-Marymount	120-101	1989
Tulsa	118-69	1989
Auburn	117-105	1994
Georgia State	117-76	1991
Delaware State	117-75	1990
Alcorn State	116-75	1995
Baylor	115-75	1990
Mississippi State	115-58	1993
Ole Miss	114-93	1992
Louisiana Tech	114-97	1991
Northeast Louisiana	114-92	1991
Texas A&M	114-100	1990
Texas Tech	113-86	1991
Texas A&M	113-88	1991
Rice	113-108	1972
Kansas State	112-88	1991
Rice	112-87	1988

HONORS

ALL-AMERICANS

1928	Glen Rose
1929	Tom Pickell, Gene Lambert
1936	Ike Poole
1941	John Adams
1977	Ron Brewer
1978	Ron Brewer, Sidney Moncrief
1979	Sidney Moncrief
1983	Darrell Walker
1984	Alvin Robertson
1991	Todd Day
1992	Todd Day
1994	Corliss Williamson
1995	Corliss Williamson

1980	Scott Hastings
1981	Scott Hastings
1982	Scott Hastings
1983	Darrell Walker
1984	Joe Kleine, Alvin Robertson
1985	Joe Kleine
1988	Ron Huery
1989	Keith Wilson
1990	Todd Day, Lee Mayberry
1991	Todd Day, Lee Mayberry, Oliver Miller

ALL-SEC

1992	Todd Day, Lee Mayberry
1993	Scotty Thurman
1994	Scotty Thurman, Corliss Williamson (Player of the Year)
1995	Scotty Thurman, Corliss Williamson (Player of the Year)

ALL-SWC

1925	Rolla Adams
1926	Rolla Adams, Elbert Pickell, Glen Rose, Curtis Parker
1927	Glen Rose, Harold Steele, Tom Pickkell
1928	Glen Rose, Tom Pickkell, Gene Lambert, Sr., Wear Schoonover
1929	Tom Pickkell, Gene Lambert, Sr., Wear Schoonover
1930	Wear Schoonover, Milan Creighton, Roy Prewitt
1931	Milan Creighton
1932	Tom Murphy, Doc Sexton
1933	Tom Murphy
1934	Taft Moody
1935	Taft Moody, Ike Poole
1936	Jim Lee Howell, Ike Poole, Elwin Gilliland
1937	Don Lockard, Jack Robbins
1938	Don Lockard, Jack Robbins
1939	Johnny Adams
1940	Howard Hickey
1941	Johnny Adams, John Freiberger, Howard Hickey
1942	R. C. Pitts
1943	Gordon Carpenter, Clayton Wynne
1944	Deno Nichols, Billy Flynt
1945	George Kok
1946	George Kok
1947	Alvin Williams
1948	George Kok
1949	Kenneth Kearns
1950	Jim Cathcart
1951	D. L. Miller
1956	Jerald Barnett, Manuel Whitely
1958	Fred Grim, Clyde Rhoden
1960	Clyde Rhoden, Pat Foster
1962	Jerry Carlton
1963	Tommy Boyer
1972	Martin Terry
1973	Martin Terry
1974	Dean Tolson
1975	Kent Allison, Robert Birden
1977	Ron Brewer, Marvin Delph, Sidney Moncrief
1978	Ron Brewer, Marvin Delph, Sidney Moncrief
1979	Sidney Moncrief

LETTERMEN

A Adams, Elmo 1950; Adams, Johnny 1939, 40, 41; Adams, O'Neal 1940, 41, 42; Adams, Marvin 1952, 53, 54; Adams, Robert 1948, 50; Adams, Rolla 1924, 25, 26; Adebayo, Sunday 1996; Allison, Kent 1975; Ambier, Robert 1949, 50, 51; Anderson, Bobby 1961, 62; Ayers, James 1926.

B Bailey, Alvin 1979; Baker, Shawn 1987, 88; Balentine, Charles 1982, 83, 84, 85; Bane, Jim 1963, 64; Barnes, Alton 1970; Barnett, Jerald 1954, 55, 56; Bass, Jody 1972, 73; Bates, Steve 1978; Beall, Elstner 1933; Beck, Corey 1993, 94, 95; Bedford, Darryl 1983, 84; Bennett, Chris 1976, 78; Benton, James 1937, 38; Biggers, Ray 1992, 93, 94; Birden, Robert 1974, 75, 76; Biley, Ken 1991, 92, 93, 94; Blackburn, Clifford 1924; Blasingame, John 1960, 61; Borgsmiller, John 1950; Boss, Ora Lee 1958, 59; Bowers, Arlyn 1989, 90, 91; Box, Larry 1972; Boyer, Tommy 1961, 62, 63; Bradley, A.B. 1942, 43; Bradley, Pat 1996; Brady, Harold 1937, 38; Brannon, Robert 1983; Brasfield, Travis 1932, 33, 34; Brewer, Ron 1976, 77, 78; Briggs, E. J. 1940; Britt, Maurice 1939; Brodie, Frank 1936, 37; Brown, Mike 1972; Brown, Tony 1979, 80, 81, 82; Bryant, Gerald 1951; Buckner, Ray 1975, 76, 77; Burk, Houston 1925, 26, 27; Butler, Walter "Pete" 1955, 56; Byles, Tony 1946, 47.

C Campbell, Doug 1972, 73; Campbell, Johnny 1947, 48; Carlton, Jerry 1960, 61, 62; Carpenter, Gordon 1941, 42, 43; Carpenter, Jay 1957, 58, 59; Carpenter, Mike 1986; Carter, Alan 1943; Cathcart, James 1948, 49, 50; Chambers, Lendon 1939; Clifton, Gus 1932; Coffman, M.B. "Skippy" 1962, 63; Coleman, Paul 1948, 49; Cook, Orval 1964, 65, 66; Cone, Benton 1967, 68, 69; Copeland, Jody 1945; Corzine, Corky 1976; Counce, Jim 1975, 76, 77, 78; Craft, Reggie 1979; Crane, Jay 1984, 85, 86; Crawford, Roger 1993, 94; Credit, Mario 1987, 88, 89, 90; Creighton, Milan 1929, 30, 31; Crockett, James 1978, 79; Cutts, Willie 1983.

D Davis, Nick 1996; Davis, Shawn 1989, 90, 91, 92; Day, Terry 1955, 56, 57; Day, Todd 1989, 90, 91, 92; DeBose, Keenan 1983, 84; Delph, Marvin 1975, 76, 77, 78; Dickson, Joe 1955, 56, 57; Dillard, Alex 1994, 1995; Donaldson, John 1938; Dunn, Wayne 1956, 57 58; Dykes, Jimmy 1982, 83, 84.

E Eidson, Harold 1929; Eldridge, James 1968, 69, 70; Elkins, Orval 1952, 53, 54; Engskov, John 1995, 96.

F Fletcher, Clyde 1991, 92; Flynt, Bill 1944, 45, 46; Foster, Pat 1959, 60, 61; Freeman, Allie 1985, 86, 87, 88; Freeman, Wally 1966, 67; Frieberger, John 1939, 40, 41; Friess, Brad 1979, 80, 81, 82; Fulton, John 1935.

G Gammill, Gerald 1939, 40; Garner, Ronnie 1959, 60, 61; Gehring, Ken 1977; Gibson, Ray 1931, 32, 33; Gilliland, Elwin 1935, 36, 37; Grim, Fred 1956, 57, 58; Grindle, LaVerne 1959, 60; Grisham, Larry 1957, 58; Grishman, Larry 1969; Guess, Charles 1965, 66.

H Hagood, Leslie 1938; Haizlip, Ralph 1927, 28; Hale, Arthur 1927, 28, 29; Hale, Harrison, Jr.

1930; Hall, Antwon 1996; Hamilton, Ray 1936, 37, 38; Hankins, Zane 1958, 59; Hastings, Scott 1979, 80, 81, 82; Hawkins, Darrell 1989, 90, 92, 93; Hays, Dennie 1936; Heider, Joel 1971, 72; Henderson, Jethro 1930; Hess, Jack 1950, 51; Hester, Bill (Toar) 1951; Hickey, Howard 1939, 40, 41; Hilliard, Keith 1980; Hogue, Larry 1962, 63, 64; Holt, Ken 1929, 30, 31; Honea, Elmer 1935; Honea, Robert 1942; Hood, Derek 1996; Horrell, Scott 1980; Horsell, J.L. 1934, 35, 36; Horst, Howard 1928; Horton, Clfford 1947, 48; Howell, Jim Lee 1934, 35, 36; Howell, Lenzie 1989, 90; Hudspeth, Gerald 1949, 50; Huery, Ron 1987, 88, 90, 91; Hurd, Anthony 1987; Hutchinson, Kenny 1985, 86, 87.

I Irvin, Byron 1985, 86.

J Jay, Jim 1963, 64; Jelks, J.L. 1931, 32, 33; Joliff, Charles 1944, 45, 46; Jones, Ben 1943, 44; Jones, Loyd 1960.

K Kays, Paul 1928; Kearns, Kenneth 1945, 46, 48; Kearns, Walter 1951, 52, 53; Keeter, Danny 1969, 70; Kelly, Carey 1980, 81, 82, 83; Kendall, Bruce 1931, 32, 33; Kimbrell, Jacky 1967, 68, 69; King, Cyrus 1924, 25; Kissee, Jim 1964, 65; Kitchen, Robert 1983, 84; Kleine, Joe 1983, 84, 85; Kok, George 1945, 46, 47, 48; Kretschmar, Joe 1956.

L Lambert, Eugene, Jr. 1951, 52, 53; Lambert, Eugene, Sr. 1928, 29; Lang, Andrew 1985, 86, 87, 88; Lee, Almer 1970, 71; Lewis, Tyron 1952; Linn, Warren 1990, 92, 93; Lively, Charels 1943; Lockard, Don 1936, 37, 38; Logue, Donald 1950; Lucas, Mike 1985; Lucke, Joe 1951, 52, 53; Lunday, Kenneth 1935, 36.

M Magness, Jim 1963, 64; Mann, Marvin 1961; Marks, Larry 1988, 89, 90; Martin, Elmer 1992, 93, 94, 95; Martin, Neal 1938, 39; Martin, Robert 1936, 37; Mayberry, Lee 1989, 90, 91, 92; McAlister, Leslie (Mack) 1968, 70; McClary, Cam 1977; McConnell, J.D. 1964, 65, 66; McDaniel, Clint 1992, 93, 94, 95; McDonald, Leo 1954, 55; McGaha, Melvin 1944, 45, 46, 47; McGuire, J.C. 1924; McKellar, Philip 1987; McKenzie, Robert 1968, 69, 70; Medlock, Rickey 1973, 74, 75; Merritt, Reggie 1993, 94, 95, 96; Miller, D. L. 1950, 51; Miller, Oliver 1989, 90, 91, 92; Mills, William 1985, 86; Mitchell, A. E. 1930; Moncrief, Sidney 1976, 77, 78, 79; Moody, Taft 1933, 34; Mooney, Fred 1970, 71; Moore, Stephan 1985, 86, 87, 88; Morris, Isaiah 1991, 92; Morrison, Alan 1960, 61; Murphy, Tom 1931, 32, 33; Murphy, Vernon 1971, 72; Murry, Ernie 1990, 91.

N Nash, Eugene 1979, 80, 81, 82; Newby, Jack 1934; Nichols, Deno 1944; Norton, Ricky 1981, 82, 83, 84; Nutt, Houston 1977.

O Oliver, Tom 1930.

P Parker, Curtis 1924, 26; Pate, Jesse 1996; Pauley, Dan 1974; Peterson, Keith 1979, 80, 81, 82; Pickell, Elbert 1924, 25, 26; Pickell, Tom 1927, 28, 29; Pickren, Jim 1929, 30, 31; Pilgrim, Lawson,

1977; Pitts, R.C. 1940, 41, 42; Poerschke, Eric 1984, 85, 86, 87; Poole, H. L. Ike 1934, 35, 36; Prewitt, Roy 1928, 29, 30; Price, Norman 1949, 50; Price, Steve 1973, 74, 75; ; ; R; ; Rankin, Roxie 1944, 47; Rankin, Tommy 1958, 59, 60; Ratliff, Mike 1984, 85, 86, 87; Ray, Herman 1935; Reed, U.S. 1978, 79, 80, 81; Reid, Kareem 1996; Rehl, Kevin 1985, 86; Renfro, Elza 1924; Rhoden, Clyde 1959, 60, 61; Richie, Ocie 1945; Rimac, Davor 1992, 93, 94, 95; Rittman, Richard 1957, 58; Robbins, Jack 1936, 37, 38; Robbins, Nobel 1941; Robertson, Alvin 1982, 83, 84; Robinson, Darnell 1994, 95, 96; Rogers, Jerry 1961, 62; Rose, Glen 1926, 27, 28; Rose, Scott 1983, 84, 85, 86; Rousseau, Steve 1964, 65, 66; Rowland, Tommy 1965, 66, 67; Rucker, Paul 1934, 35; Ruckman, Charles 1925, 26.

S Sagely, Floyd 1952, 53, 54; Sailer, Bill 1952, 53; Saulsberry, Daryll 1975, 76; Schall, Steve 1976, 77, 78, 79; Schoonover, Wear 1928, 29, 30; Schulte, Jack 1974, 75, 76; Schumchyk, Frank 1944, 45, 46; Schumchyk, Mike 1944, 45, 46; Scott, David 1979; Scott, Darryl 1985, 86; Scott, Tim 1987, 88; Scroggins, Carroll 1953, 54, 55; Searles, John 1971; Self, David 1966, 67, 68; Self, Jewell 1959; Sexton, Doc 1931, 32, 33; Shaw, Raymond 1952, 53, 54; Shepherd, Robert 1992, 93; Sims, Keith 1944; Skulman, Greg 1980, 81, 82; Smith, Buddy 1954, 55, 56; Smith, Glenn 1939; Smith, Norman 1954, 55, 56; Smith, Sammy 1950, 51, 52; Sneed, Brice 1959; Snively, John 1982, 83; Southerland, Billy 1940; Spears, Roger 1972, 73, 74; Steele, Harold 1925, 26, 27; Stephens, Gary 1967, 68; Stewart, Dwight 1993, 94, 95; Stolzer, Lawrence 1957, 58; Stroud, Steve

1976, 77; Sugg, Ricky 1964, 65, 66; Sutton, Leroy 1980, 82, 83, 84.

T Talkington, John 1964, 65, 67; Tanneberger, Ricky 1968, 69, 70; Terry, Charles 1975, 76; Thompson, Ali 1996; Thompson, Harry 1957, 58, 59; Thurman, Scotty 1993, 94, 95; Tolson, Dean 1972, 73, 74; Towns, Marlon 1996; Trapp, Charles 1930; Trumbo, Donald 1956; Trumbo, Trey 1976, 77; Tuck, Henry 1937.

V Vint, Bobby 1968, 70, 71; Vogel, Warren 1963, 64.

W Walker, Darrell 1981, 82, 83; Walker, J.W. 1952; Wallace, Roosevelt 1991, 92; Waller, P. T. "Duddy" 1951; Watts, Donnie 1969, 71; West, James 1950; Wheeler, Paul 1944, 45, 46; Whitby, Cannon 1987, 88, 89, 90; White, Dennis 1972, 73, 74; Whitley, Manuel 1950, 53; Williams, Alvin 1946, 47, 48; Williams, Robert 1949, 50, 51; Williamson, Corliss 1993, 94, 95; Wilson, Jessie 1942, 43; Wilson, Jim 1962, 63; Wilson, Keith 1987, 88, 89; Wilson, Lee 1994, 1995,1996; Windle, James 1959; Wooford, Larry 1961, 62, 63; Wynne, Clayton 1941, 42, 43.

Y Young, Ott 1942; Young, Mike 1978, 79, 80, 81.

Z Zahn, Alan 1977, 78, 79, 80.

TRIVIA ANSWERS

1. Glen Rose.

2. Northeast Oklahoma State, 19-11 and 33-12 in 1923-24.

3. Ricky Medlock, .939 in 1974-75.

4. 166 against U.S. International in a Dec. 9, 1989, game in Barnhill Arena.

5. Lee Mayberry, 139 in 1988-1992.

6. A 117-66 loss to Ole Miss on Dec. 10, 1973.

7. Tom Pickell and Gene Lambert.

8. Mike Conley.

9. The Razorbacks won three straight before losing to Schmidt's TCU cagers.

10. The 1990-91 team averaged an astounding 99.6 points per game.

11. Tim Scott, 11.9.

12. Most points ever in a NCAA Midwest Regional game.

13. A 131-109 win over Baylor in 1972.

14. Tolson took 36 shots against Texas A&M.

15. Martin Terry, 26.3, 1972-73.

16. 84.

17. Charles Corgan.

18. 25, from 1923-24 to 1947-48.

19. 82 vs. Bethune Cookman (Arkansas 128, Bethune Cookman 46 on Dec. 4, 1991).

20. 117 in a 117-105 win at Auburn on Jan. 15, 1994.

21. Four turnovers vs. Texas on Feb. 2, 1980.

22. Alvin Robertson.

23. They have won 24 SWC and SEC titles.

24. 1957.

25. Eugene "The Dunking Machine" Nash, who played from 1979-82.

26. Three of Arkansas six Final Four appearances came before the 1990s (1941, 1945, 1978).

27. Richardson had brief tryouts with the AFL's San Diego Chargers and the ABA's Dallas Chapparals.

28. The St. Louis Cardinals.

29. A 17-11 loss to SMU in 1923-24.

30. 10 games during the 1970-71 season.

31. Todd Day with 2,395 points from 1988-92.

32. 104.

33. Dean Tolson, 12.4 in 1972-73.

34. In a 166-101 win over U.S. International in 1990.

35. Dwight Stewart

36. Lawrence Moten, who called a timeout that his team didn't have resulting in a technical foul and giving Arkansas an opportunity to tie the second-round game and send it into overtime.

37. 4-2.

38. 11.

39. Alan Zahn.

40. 31-3.

41. $35 million.

42. John Barnhill.

43. Arkansas' 92-47 win over Houston in 1975-76.

44. Billy "Toar" Hester, who played varsity basketball in 1951 before transferring to Centenary.

45. A school record 75.

46. 37-22.

47. 7.

48. 104 over Texas Christian.

49. A title at the Little Rock Classic in 1969.

50. 98-14.

COLLEGE SPORTS HANDBOOKS

Stories, Stats & Stuff About America's Favorite Teams

U. of Arizona	Basketball	Arizona Wildcats Handbook
Baylor	Football	Bears Handbook
Clemson	Football	Clemson Handbook
U. of Colorado	Football	Buffaloes Handbook
U. of Florida	Football	Gator Tales
Georgia Tech	Basketball	Yellow Jackets Handbook
Indiana U.	Basketball	Hoosier Handbook
Iowa State	Sports	Cyclones Handbook
U. of Kansas	Basketball	Crimson & Blue Handbook
Kansas State	Sports	Kansas St Wildcat Handbook
LSU	Football	Fighting Tigers Handbook
U. of Louisville	Basketball	Cardinals Handbook
U. of Miami	Football	Hurricane Handbook
U. of Michigan	Football	Wolverines Handbook
U. of Missouri	Basketball	Tiger Handbook
U. of Nebraska	Football	Husker Handbook
U. of N. Carolina	Basketball	Tar Heels Handbook
N.C. State	Basketball	Wolfpack Handbook
U. of Oklahoma	Football	Sooners Handbook
Penn State	Football	Nittany Lions Handbook
U. of S. Carolina	Football	Gamecocks Handbook
Stanford	Football	Stanford Handbook
Syracuse	Sports	Orange Handbook
U. of Tennessee	Football	Volunteers Handbook
U. of Texas	Football	Longhorns Handbook
Texas A&M	Football	Aggies Handbook
Texas Tech	Sports	Red Raiders Handbook
Virginia Tech	Football	Hokies Handbook
Wichita State	Sports	Shockers Handbook
U. of Wisconsin	Football	Badgers Handbook

Also:

Big 12 Handbook: Stories, Stats and Stuff About The Nation's Best
    Football Conference
The Top Fuel Handbook: Stories, Stats and Stuff About Drag Racing's
    Most Powerful Class

For ordering information call Midwest Sports Publications at: